"Murali and Venkatesan's close examination of infertility comics, or 'gynographics,' confirms what proponents of graphic medicine have long known: comics are a powerful space for silenced voices to, finally, be heard."

Matthew Noe, *Harvard Medical School, USA*

"Combining an acute analysis of the often conflicting medical and socio-cultural constructions of infertility with illuminating, theoretically informed readings of four trailblazing works of graphic medicine, this book will be a valuable addition to courses in Feminist and Women's Studies, Medical Humanities, History of Medicine, and Comics Studies. More than that, this will engage the mind and heart of anyone who has faced the challenging experience of infertility."

Susan Squier, *Brill Professor Emerita of Women's, Gender, and Sexuality Studies and English, The Pennsylvania State University, USA*

Infertility Comics and Graphic Medicine

Infertility Comics and Graphic Medicine examines women's graphic memoirs on infertility, foregrounding the complex interrelationship between women's life writing, infertility studies, and graphic medicine.

Through a scholarly examination of the artists' use of visual-verbal codes of the comics medium in narrating their physical ordeals and affective challenges occasioned by infertility, the book seeks to foreground the intricacies of gender identity, embodiment, subjectivity, and illness experience. Providing long-overdue scholarly attention on the perspectives of autobiographical and comics studies, the authors examine the gendered nature of the infertility experience and the notion of motherhood as an ideological force which interpolates socio-cultural discourses, accentuating the potential of graphic medicine as a creative space for the infertile women to voice their hitherto silenced perspectives on childlessness with force and urgency.

This interdisciplinary volume will be of interest to scholars and students in comics studies, the health humanities, literature, and women's and gender studies, and will also be suitable for readers in visual studies and narrative medicine.

Chinmay Murali was a Senior Research Fellow in the Department of Humanities and Social Sciences at the National Institute of Technology, Trichy, India. He is currently an independent researcher. His research interests include literature and medicine, graphic medicine, and critical health humanities. His research articles have appeared in *Perspectives in Biology and Medicine*, *Journal of Medical Humanities*, *Journal of Graphic Novels and Comics*, *Women's Studies*, among others. He is a recipient of the Visiting Scholar fellowship from the Center for Health Humanities, MCPHS University, Boston, USA.

Sathyaraj Venkatesan is Associate Professor of English in the Department of Humanities and Social Sciences at the National Institute of Technology, Trichy, India. He is the author of six books and over 90 research publications that span African American literature, health humanities, graphic medicine, film studies, and other literary and cultural studies disciplines. He is most recently co-author of *Gender, Eating Disorders and Graphic Medicine* and *India Retold*.

Routledge Focus on Gender, Sexuality, and Comics
Series Editor: Frederik Byrn Køhlert, University of East Anglia

Routledge Focus on Gender, Sexuality, and Comics publishes original short-form research in the areas of gender and sexuality studies as they relate to comics cultures past and present. Topics in the series cover printed as well as digital media, mainstream and alternative comics industries, transmedia adaptions, comics consumption, and various comics-associated cultural fields and forms of expression. Gendered and sexual identities are considered as intersectional and always in conversation with issues concerning race, ethnicity, ability, class, age, nationality, and religion.

Books in the series are between 25,000 and 45,000 words and can be single-authored, co-authored, or edited collections. For longer works, the companion series "Routledge Studies in Gender, Sexuality, and Comics" publishes full-length books between 60,000 to 90,000 words.

Series editor Frederik Byrn Køhlert is a lecturer in American Studies at the University of East Anglia, where he is also the coordinator of the Master of Arts program in Comics Studies. In addition to several journal articles and book chapters on comics, he is the author of *Serial Selves: Identity and Representation in Autobiographical Comics*.

Cosplayers
Gender and Identity
A. Luxx Mishou

Gender and Sexuality in Israeli Graphic Novels
Matt Reingold

Infertility Comics and Graphic Medicine
Chinmay Murali and Sathyaraj Venkatesan

www.routledge.com/Routledge-Focus-on-Gender-Sexuality-and-Comics-Studies/book-series/FGSC

Infertility Comics and Graphic Medicine

Chinmay Murali and
Sathyaraj Venkatesan

LONDON AND NEW YORK

First published 2022
by Routledge
2 Park Square, Milton Park, Abingdon, Oxon OX14 4RN

and by Routledge
605 Third Avenue, New York, NY 10158

Routledge is an imprint of the Taylor & Francis Group, an informa business

© 2022 Chinmay Murali and Sathyaraj Venkatesan

The right of Chinmay Murali and Sathyaraj Venkatesan to be identified as authors of this work has been asserted by them in accordance with sections 77 and 78 of the Copyright, Designs and Patents Act 1988.

All rights reserved. No part of this book may be reprinted or reproduced or utilised in any form or by any electronic, mechanical, or other means, now known or hereafter invented, including photocopying and recording, or in any information storage or retrieval system, without permission in writing from the publishers.

Trademark notice: Product or corporate names may be trademarks or registered trademarks, and are used only for identification and explanation without intent to infringe.

British Library Cataloguing-in-Publication Data
A catalogue record for this book is available from the British Library

Library of Congress Cataloging-in-Publication Data
A catalog record has been requested for this book

ISBN: 978-0-367-46415-8 (hbk)
ISBN: 978-1-032-07739-0 (pbk)
ISBN: 978-1-003-02862-8 (ebk)

DOI: 10.4324/9781003028628

Typeset in Times New Roman
by Newgen Publishing UK

Contents

List of figures ix
Acknowledgements x

Introduction 1
Graphic medicine and gynographics: discipline, discourse, and perspectives 2
Infertility: defining a global problem 3
Is infertility a disease? 4
Infertility and gender 5
Data for analysis 8
Aims, objectives, and methodology 8
Overview of the book 10

1 Visualising illness: comics and graphic medicine 15
Introduction 15
Humanising healthcare: from medical humanities to health humanities 16
Narrative medicine: legitimising the patient's perspective 19
Autopathography, graphic pathography, and life writing 21
Comics, graphic medicine, and women's life writing 23
Graphic medicine as a pedagogical tool 25
Graphic medicine as therapy, community, and critique 27
Internationalisation and popularisation of graphic medicine 29
Conclusion 31

2 Imagining "the barren": cultural representations of women's infertility 35
Introduction 35
Illness and representations 36

Infertile women in popular novels and mass-market women's magazines 38
  Self-blame and neurosis in TV melodramas 40
  Egg-freezing ads and the rhetoric of choice 42
  Infertile monsters in reality TV, and horror films 43
  Countering infertile subjectivity in women's memoirs 45
  Conclusion 47

3 Hegemonic creations: pronatalism and the social construction of motherhood 52
  Introduction 52
  Pronatalism and the social construction of motherhood 52
  "NO! THIS way!": girl child as a pronatalist subject 55
  "We're in the club!": childlessness and cultural otherhood 60
  "Let me out!": thinking beyond motherhood 64
  Conclusion 68

4 The infertile body in the clinic: medicalisation and loss of agency 71
  Introduction 71
  Feminist critique of medicalisation 71
  "The infertility death trap": Broken Eggs *and* Present/Perfect *76*
  "Der straightener Herr Doktor": The Facts of Life *and* Good Eggs *83*
  Conclusion 87

5 Traversing infertility: endurance and alternatives 91
  Introduction 91
  Resilience, coping, and infertile subjectivity 91
  Spiritual and creative coping in Good Eggs *94*
  Art, ecology, and alternative mothering practices in The Facts of Life *97*
  Conclusion 102

  Conclusion 106

  Index 111

Figures

3.1	Paula Knight, *The Facts of Life* (Myriad, 2017), 18	55
3.2	Paula Knight, *The Facts of Life* (Myriad, 2017), 19	59
3.3	Paula Knight, *The Facts of Life* (Myriad, 2017), 205	63
3.4	Paula Knight, *The Facts of Life* (Myriad, 2017), 227	68
4.1	Emily Steinberg, *Broken Eggs* (Cleaver, 2014). n.p	77
4.2	Emily Steinberg, *Broken Eggs* (Cleaver, 2014). n.p	80
4.3	Paula Knight, *The Facts of Life* (Myriad, 2017), 85	85
5.1	Paula Knight, *The Facts of Life* (Myriad, 2017), 214	100

Acknowledgements

Chinmay Murali

I am indebted to my research adviser, Dr Sathyaraj Venkatesan, for teaching me the nuances of literary research and academic writing. Dr Venkatesan's mentorship has enormously helped me in recognising the value of diligence and professionalism in academia. I thank the Routledge editorial team: Frederik Byrn Køhlert and Alexandra McGregor for their trust, valuable comments, and generosity; Eleanor Simmons for her assistance during manuscript preparation. I am extremely grateful to Professor Dien Ho and the Center for Health Humanities, MCPHS University, Boston, for the Visiting Scholar fellowship. Many thanks to Paula Knight, Emily Steinberg, Phoebe Potts, and Jenell Johnson for their prompt responses and insightful comments. Particularly, I would like to thank Knight and Steinberg for graciously allowing me to reproduce their art in my book. Special thanks to my colleagues and friends at the National Institute of Technology, Trichy. A word of gratitude to my parents, my in-laws, Dr Mohankumar and Dr Sheela, and my siblings, Chinthak and Chiranmay. They have been a source of unflinching support and cheer. Much love to my wife, Parvathy Madhavi, whose company and inputs made my research work less daunting.

Sathyaraj Venkatesan

Many thanks to my PhD graduate students. The book has immensely benefited from their conversations, seminars, and class presentations over many years. They are my strength. I would also like to acknowledge the support of International Graphic Medicine collective: M. K. Czerwiec, Ian Williams, Susan Merrill Squier, Matthew Noe, A. David Lewis, Michael Green, and Brian C. Callender. I owe a special debt of gratitude to my teachers, Professor Gurumurthy Neelakantan (Indian Institute of Technology, Kanpur) and Dr Vijay Nair for stretching my imagination in decisive ways. Special thanks to Frederik Byrn Køhlert and Alexandra McGregor for their sensitive guidance during the preparation of the manuscript. I am also grateful to the reviewers for their thoughtful critiques and valuable suggestions. Special thanks are due to the faculty of the Department of Humanities and Social Sciences, National Institute of Technology (NIT), Tiruchirappalli, and my family, Pavithra Ayyapan and Taran Sathyaraj.

Introduction

In August of 2019, Rasu Jayabalan, an Assistant Professor at the National Institute of Technology, Rourkela (India), and his wife Malvi Kesavan committed suicide. According to the couple's friends and family, the suicide was shocking since the deceased "seemed like any other couple, with no sign of any major distress coming through" (Ann 2019). However, the couple's suicide note mentions distress over not being able to have a child as the cause of the suicide. The suicide of Jayabalan and his wife illustrates the mental agony, and cultural shame attached to infertility, forcing couples to suffer in silence. In fact, pronatal discourses and ideologies that valorise maternity, childbearing, and pregnancy even censor conversations surrounding reproductive disorders and failures. Former US first lady, Michelle Obama, for instance, in her memoir *Becoming* (2018) describes how such cultural censoring not only isolates the sufferers but also aggravates their predicament. Citing her personal experience, Obama observes: "I felt lost and alone and I felt like I'd failed … because we don't talk about them [reproductive failures]" (Obama 2018). Recently, Meghan Markle, Duchess of Sussex, echoed Obama's sentiment when she recounted her struggles with miscarriage thus: "despite the staggering commonality of this pain, the conversation remains taboo, riddled with (unwarranted) shame, and perpetuating a cycle of solitary mourning" (Markle 2020). There exists a deafening cultural silence surrounding infertility and other related reproductive circumstances which makes it difficult for the sufferers to even voice their tribulations.

In this context, personal narratives on reproductive failures in which the sufferers voice their lived and experiential realities attain significance. Such narratives not only lend voice to the sufferers' agony but also claim cultural legitimacy and visibility for issues which have hitherto been silenced and marginalised. Notably, an emerging body of graphic medicine memoirs addresses nuanced issues centred on women's infertility

DOI: 10.4324/9781003028628-1

and its attendant personal, socio-cultural, and medical challenges. Here it is apposite to examine the emerging discourse of graphic medicine in relation to women's graphic memoirs on infertility and other related reproductive health quandaries.

Graphic medicine and gynographics: discipline, discourse, and perspectives

Graphic medicine is an emerging interdisciplinary field that combines the concerns of comics and the discourses of healthcare and medicine. M. K. Czerwiec, one of the key practitioners of the field, defines graphic medicine as "the intersection of the medium of comics and the discourse of healthcare" (Czerwiec et al. 2015, 1). Partly inspired by the subversive legacy of the underground comix, graphic medicine explores tabooed themes and marginal perspectives "that escape both the normal realms of medicine and the comforts of canonical literature" (Squier 2008, 130). As such, graphic medicine narratives (or graphic pathographies) redraw the contours of the medical discourse by recognising the centrality of the patients' voice which has hitherto been marginalised. The medium of comics is considered as performing a critical function in this enterprise because it is "an important deconstructive and revolutionary medium in the 20th century" (Schmitt 1992, 153). Put differently, "comics have often been associated with cultural changes and are ideal for exploring taboo or forbidden areas of illness and healthcare" (Czerwiec et al. 2015, 3).

Mostly autobiographical and patient-produced, graphic pathographies explore diverse themes such as patient identity, the doctor–patient relationship, challenges of caregiving, the industrialisation and commercialisation of health care, death and grieving, complementary and alternative medicine, among others. Graphic medicine narratives that have received critical acclaim include Brian Fies' *Mom's Cancer* (2006), Ken Dahl's *Monsters* (2009), David Small's *Stitches* (2010), Ian Williams' *The Bad Doctor* (2014), and Georgia Webber's *Dumb: Living without a Voice* (2018), among others. Interestingly, there is a proliferation of graphic medicine narratives centred on the quandaries of women's reproduction such as infertility, miscarriage, abortion, and post-partum depression. Among such narratives are Phoebe Potts' *Good Eggs* (2010), Endrene Shepherd's *A Significant Loss: The Story of My Miscarriage* (2014), Ryan Alexander-Tanner and Jessica Zucker's *Overwhelmed, Anxious and Angry: Navigating Postpartum Depression* (2015), and Paula Knight's *The Facts of Life* (2017), with the most recent addition being *Menopause: A Comic Treatment* (2020) edited by M. K. Czerwiec. These narratives are peculiar in that they address nuanced and often silenced issues centred on the complexities of female reproduction from a uniquely subjective and lived perspective.

In this context, we propose a term "gynographics" to denote visual narratives that centre on female reproductive quandaries. Etymologically, the term evolves from "gyno" which means relating to women/female reproduction and "graphics" which connotes images or visual representations. "Gynographics" may be conceived as an addition to critical vocabulary on female-centric literary/theoretical approaches with similar terminologies such as "gynocriticism" and "gynocentrism." While "gynocriticism" was a term coined by feminist critic Elaine Showalter in the 1970s to foreground the need to have a uniquely female framework in the analysis of texts authored by women, "gynocentrism" has been in theoretical parlance as a term that encapsulates female-centric perspectives or the advocacy of it. Though gynographics is related to the aforementioned terms in its attention on "the female," it particularly focuses on a unique aspect of feminine experience, i.e., reproduction. In a similar vein, as a subgenre of graphic medicine, gynographics is related yet different from women's comics in general and comics/visual narratives that address other female health quandaries such as breast cancer and eating disorders.

This book examines select autobiographical gynographics (or women's graphic memoirs) on infertility, demonstrating the gendered realities of involuntary childlessness. The book further explores how subjective and personalised articulations of childlessness enable infertile women to register the lived and phenomenological dimensions of their suffering. Foregrounding the situated and embodied nature of the infertility experience, these memoirists visualise the complex affective states and social stress that the infertile subject is constantly forced to negotiate every day. Finally, the study argues that these infertility memoirs are culturally significant in that they accord a voice and visibility to an otherwise stigmatised women's health quandary.

Infertility: defining a global problem

Infertility is a gender-neutral health problem which affects both men and women. Clinically, it is "a disease of the reproductive system defined by the failure to achieve a clinical pregnancy after 12 months or more of regular unprotected sexual intercourse" (WHO 2009). Put differently, infertility is "the inability of a sexually active, non-contracepting couple to achieve pregnancy in one year" (WHO 2009). When a couple is unable to reproduce due to medical problems that lie with the male partner, the condition is referred to as male infertility. Male infertility includes "any health issue in a man that lowers the chances of his female partner getting pregnant" (Urology Care, n.d.). Women's infertility, on the other hand, is defined as "not being able to get pregnant after one year of trying (or six months if a woman is 35 or older)" (Office on Women's Health 2017). Women who can get pregnant yet are unable to sustain their pregnancy are also categorised as infertile.

Women's infertility is classified as primary and secondary infertility. A woman is considered as having primary infertility when she is "unable to ever bear a child, either due to the inability to become pregnant or the inability to carry a pregnancy to a live birth" (WHO 2009). In technical terms, primary infertility is defined as "the absence of a live birth for women who desire a child and have been in a union for at least five years, during which they have not used any contraceptives" (Mascarenhas et al. 2012). Hence those women "whose pregnancy spontaneously miscarries, or whose pregnancy results in a still born child, without ever having had a live birth" would be treated as experiencing primary infertility (WHO 2009). Secondary infertility, on the other hand, is "the absence of a live birth for women who desire a child and have been in a union for at least five years since their last live birth, during which they did not use any contraceptives" (Mascarenhas et al. 2012). In short, despite trying, women who are unable to have a live birth following a previous pregnancy which has resulted in a live birth is considered as suffering from secondary infertility. Statistically, infertility affects "an estimated 48.5 million couples worldwide" (Mascarenhas et al. 2012), attesting to the global impact of the problem. While "around 10 percent of women aged 15 to 44 years are estimated to have difficulty conceiving or staying pregnant" in the US alone (Nordqvist 2018), infertility has been found to affect one in every four couples in developing countries (WHO 2012). Evidently, infertility is a pressing health issue (affecting both men and women) whose global impact cannot be understated.

Is infertility a disease?

As a health condition, infertility is neither life-threatening nor physically debilitating. It becomes a pressing concern only when the couple desires to have children and those who choose to be childfree might not even recognise whether they are infertile or not. Nevertheless, the desire to have a biological child and the inability to reproduce can constitute intense psychic turmoil in the sufferer. Interestingly, the longing to beget children, the psychological suffering that accompanies the failure to procreate, and the subsequent reliance on medicine for cure are mediated by pronatal socio-cultural discourses including family, religion, media, and the medical discourse. Pronatal cultural discourses categorise infertility as a disease that requires medical intervention. Cultural expectations on men and women to reproduce, perpetuated by pronatal discourses and ideologies of motherhood, mandate infertile couples to perceive infertility as a deviance that needs to be medically treated.

Additionally, the role of the discourse of medicine in framing infertility as a serious disease that require a medical remedy cannot be understated. As medical anthropologists Gay Becker and Robert D. Nachtigall argue, "[a]lthough infertility is not a disease, it is treated like one in the health care system" (1992, 458). Framing infertility as a "condition that has recently been recast as a disease" (457), Becker and Nachtigall critique the medicalisation of the condition. In fact, biomedicine internalises, sustains, and reproduces pronatal socio-cultural mandates and deems infertility as a disease that must be cured. This pathologising and medicalisation of infertility illustrates how "the health care system reflects the same value system at work throughout society" (Becker and Nachtigall 1992, 456). At another level, the medicalisation of infertility and the subsequent mushrooming of fertility clinics form part of an ever-greater medicalisation of ordinary human conditions, including menopause, male pattern baldness, and obesity. With the annual healthcare spending on these common conditions in the US touching $77.1 billion in 2005 (Conrad et al. 2010), this trend reflects the significance of medicalising infertility in the context of marketisation and commercialisation of contemporary healthcare systems.

Infertility and gender

Despite infertility being a gender-neutral health predicament, women are mostly blamed for the couple's childlessness even when their partner has fertility issues. Moreover, the cultural valorisation of motherhood and the uncritical entwining of maternity and femininity cause severe psychic harm to childless women. The failure to fulfil the cultural mandate of motherhood profoundly impacts women's perception of the self and identity, and they are perceived as a stigmatised category within the local moral worlds to which they belong. As Elaine May (1997) contends, "[t]he fact that reproduction remains primarily a woman's problem is due less to their biological capacity for pregnancy, and more to the cultural norms that still place motherhood at the centre of female identity" (32).

Further, commenting on the gendered nature of the infertility experience and its psycho-social consequences on the female gender, Frank van Balen and Marcia C. Inhorn (2002) observe that women across the globe "bear the major burden of infertility, in terms of the blame for the reproductive failing; personal anxiety, frustration, grief, and fear; marital duress, dissolution and abandonment; social stigma and community ostracism; and, in some cases, life-threatening medical interventions" (7). In a similar vein, Robin E. Jensen (2016) in her study on the rhetorical constructions of infertility titled *Infertility: History of a Transformative Term* observes that, though men and their bodies have a central role in the process of reproduction, women have "remained the primary focus of medical and societal discussions about barrenness, sterility and infertility" (8).

The socio-cultural experience of infertility across cultures has been profoundly shaped by patriarchal notions and misogynistic attitudes which perpetuate gendered cultural norms and values that are detrimental to women. For instance, in Egypt women are made to bear the stigma of childlessness even when the problem is with the male partner (Inhorn 2002), while in "Bangladeshi slums the 'treatment' for males is remarriage, as women are held responsible for infertility" (Greil et al. 2011, 740). Similarly, in India, "irrespective of the cause behind a couple's childlessness, women by default carry a greater load of blame, responsibility, and guilt for reproductive failures" (Patel et al. 2018). In developed countries such as the US, "media often constructs the typical infertility patient as a middle-class White woman who delayed childbearing in order to pursue a career" (Greil et al. 2011, 738). Evidently, framing infertility as a woman's problem and holding women responsible for the condition is a cross-cultural phenomenon.

Tracing the social construction of the experience of infertility historically, Jensen argues that, long before the twentieth century, the cause of women's infertility was "attributed to immorality, sexual perversion, strenuous intellectual work, and so-called masculine aspirations" (2016, 6). In a similar vein, Margarete J. Sandelowski (1990) observes that the perception that women are to be held responsible for increasing infertility among married couples "emerged in the latter decades of the nineteenth century when increasing public attention was directed toward women's new educational and occupational aspirations, their assertions of independence and claim to political rights" (482). Jensen clarifies how such misogynistic and patriarchal perceptions of infertility coerced the childless married women to "undergo painful sessions of bloodletting and surgery without anaesthesia, forgo education and professional opportunities, and, whenever possible, avoid work outside the home"

(2016, 6). In the twentieth and twenty-first centuries, Jensen contends that women's experience of infertility is systematically mediated by increased medicalisation and technological interventions: "women who are deemed 'infertile' face nothing less than a technological mandate to alter their behaviour – sometimes endlessly – to achieve pregnancy and parenthood" (6–7).

Surprisingly, the discourse of biomedicine has been no less gendered in its conceptualisations of infertility. Citing evidences from J. S. Haller and R. M. Haller's *The Physician and Sexuality in Victorian America* (1974), Sandelowski (1990) argues that a recurrent theme in the medical literature on women's fertility was that "expanded education and women's ambitions perverted their biological destiny" (485). As such, marital infertility was conceptualised by macho biomedicine as "a social disease, a disorder of civilization and modern living, involving culpable, largely female acts of omission and commission" (1990, 485), which implied that women delaying conception because of their intellectual pursuits and career aspirations was the primary reason for increasing infertility among couples. Illustrating the fact that contemporary biomedicine continues to be misogynistic and macho in its treatment of infertility, Elaine May (1997) notes that women's "bodies are likely to be the ones poked, prodded and pumped with hormones, even if they are fertile and the problem resides with the male partner" (31). As Arthur Greil observes, [r]regardless of which partner has a 'problem,' it is the woman who is the focus of most infertility treatment" (2002, 101). Moreover, in fertility clinics, women's bodies are subjected to (often unnecessary) technological and medical gaze where they are treated like objects/machines, resulting in the experience of depersonalisation and objectification. In sum, though infertility is a health issue which affects all genders, it is women who are most often blamed, stigmatised, and victimised, both socio-culturally and medically, making the lived experience of infertility a gendered one. To quote Greil, "[t]he simultaneously biological, personal, and social drama of infertility is played out in the woman's body" (2002, 101).

Although the socio-cultural challenges of infertility affect women more, men also experience social stigma in being unable to attain parenthood. As Liberty Walther Barnes notes, "across cultures, the ideal macho man is depicted as virile and potent" and there exists a "prevailing cultural belief that healthy testicles producing potent sperm are symbols of strength, courage, power, manliness, and masculinity" (Barnes 2014, 4). This cultural expectation of masculinity not only fractures infertile men's selfhood and identity but also creates intense emotional turmoil in them.

Data for analysis

This study examines the following graphic medicine narratives on female infertility: *Present/Perfect* (2018) by Jenell Johnson, *The Facts of Life* (2017) by Paula Knight, *Broken Eggs* (2014) by Emily Steinberg, and *Good Eggs* (2010) by Phoebe Potts. These narratives could be broadly categorised as graphic memoirs on female infertility. Interestingly, all these works are authored by established comics artists, with Jenell Johnson's *Present/Perfect* being the only exception since Johnson is an academic by profession. Except Paula Knight who grew up in North-East England and works in Bristol, other authors chosen for this study are of American origin, almost all currently settled and working in the US. While the artwork, narrative techniques, themes, and perspectives vary in each of these narratives, they nevertheless foreground the gendered and lived realities of experiencing infertility.

Aims, objectives, and methodology

Considering the gravity of infertility as a pressing health problem with socio-cultural underpinnings, the theme of female infertility and other reproductive quandaries from the perspective of autobiographical and comics studies has not been given enough scholarly attention. This book scrutinises women's graphic memoirs on infertility, bringing into relief the intricacies of the complex interrelationship between women's life writing, infertility studies, and graphic medicine. Primarily, the book aims to explore how visual memoirists use the pluripotent space of the comics medium and its affordances to foreground the gendered nature of their infertility experience. In so doing, the study attempts a critique of pronatalism as an ideological force which interpolates mainstream discourses, in the process scrutinising the socio-cultural othering and stigma associated with non-motherhood. Additionally, the book investigates the misogynistic tendencies that characterise the medicalisation of female infertility which deprives patients of their bodily autonomy and agency. Finally, the study explores how authors positively navigate their predicament of childlessness through their unique coping practices, thereby accepting their non-mother identity. The study not only underscores the significance of women's memoirs as a counter-discourse to the essentialising and stereotypical mainstream representations of women's infertility but also accentuates the potential of graphic medicine in according cultural visibility and legitimacy to women's non-mother identity.

Introduction 9

Here, it is instructive to consider the positionality of the authors of this study in relation to the topic of research. As male researchers from the global south who are professionally trained in the interdisciplinary fields of graphic medicine, health humanities, and gender studies, we are sensitive to the cultural and social realities of women, specifically in the context of health and illness. Our constant engagement with health humanities and graphic medicine has enabled us to recognise women's infertility as an understudied yet significant health issue that deserves an in-depth analysis. Inferences in this book are based on qualitative research and descriptive close readings of the chosen texts. While the absence of graphic medicine narratives on women's infertility from our immediate cultural context has forced us to rely more on graphic memoirs from the US and the UK, we have included in this study experiences of infertile women from our cultural context through secondary sources and other media. We recognise that men's experience of infertility also deserves attention from the perspective of graphic medicine, however, there is only one graphic memoir on male infertility, William Roy's *In vitro* (2014). Because of the absence of graphic medicine accounts from other ethnic groups, this study has also limited its attention to white women's experience of childlessness. The experience of infertility among queer/LGBTQ communities is also absent in graphic medicine. With the gradual emergence and popularity of graphic medicine in non-western settings in the future, further research in this area can focus on memoirs authored by men, sexual minorities, and non-white ethnic groups.

This study largely follows two reading modes that are widely deployed in the analysis of comics and graphic novels: (a) McCloud's approach, and (b) Groensteen's approach. Inspired by Will Eisner's characterisation of comics as sequential art in his *Comics and Sequential Art*, comics theorist Scott McCloud (1994) defines comics as "juxtaposed pictorial and other images in deliberate sequence" (9) which emphasises the sequential relationship between fundamental elements in comics. French comics theorist Thierry Groensteen, on the other hand, advocates the method of treating comics as a network where constituent elements exist in linear and non-linear relationship with one another. This study adopts a methodological framework which deploys both McCloud's and Groensteen's theoretical models in its analysis of comics. The panels are analysed in their sequential relation with one another, a method McCloud proposes in his *Understanding Comics: The Invisible Art* (1994). Apart from this McCloudian approach, the method of analysing panels in relation to other unrelated panels which together form the constituent elements of larger units or grand articulations, a method Groensteen advocates in his *The System of Comics* (2007), is also adopted. Following a qualitative approach, close reading is deployed for formal and content analyses of the primary texts chosen. Additionally, an attempt is also made to explore how the comics form contributes to the content and the interaction of words and images in creating the textual meaning. In short, the study illustrates the arguments through an analysis of panel(s) and pages from multiple texts, exploring their nuances through close reading.

Overview of the book

Each chapter of this book investigates the topic of discussion from diverse perspectives, thereby contributing to the central argument that graphic medicine accords a creative space for women to visualise their gendered and stigmatised experiences of infertility. The book is divided into five chapters, excluding the Introduction and Conclusion. Chapter 1 offers a general overview of graphic medicine in its generic contexts, focusing on how the medium of comics offers a visual-verbal vocabulary to discourses on health and illness. The chapter not only establishes the field of graphic medicine as an offshoot of the medical/health humanities movement but also identifies the influential role of narrative medicine in shaping the central tenets and concerns of this emerging interdisciplinary area. The chapter focuses on the disruptive potential of graphic medicine in furthering the aims of health humanities and narrative medicine to develop a patient-centred and value-based discourse on medicine and healthcare. At another level, this chapter identifies the growing corpus of graphic autopathographies as a significant addition to life narratives on illness, arguing that visual memoirs enrich life writing's scope of narrativising the ill self. Special emphasis is laid on how women's autopathographies enable sufferers to externalise their lived and subjective perspectives on the gendered nature of illness experiences. The chapter also scrutinises graphic medicine as a critique of biomedicine. Graphic medicine's power in creating awareness, building communities of sufferers, and offering cathartic relief to artists is also examined in detail. The chapter concludes by acknowledging the growing popularity and globality of graphic medicine as an emerging interdisciplinary approach to health, illness, and medicine.

Chapter 2 explores the popular cultural representations of women's infertility, illustrating how such imaginings reinforce dominant stereotypes and erroneous perceptions surrounding the problem. Examining

Introduction 11

diverse popular cultural texts, spread across various media and genres such as women's magazines, novels, advertisements, TV melodramas, horror films, and reality TV shows, this section lays bare the politics of representation in the context of female infertility. Finally, the chapter demonstrates how women's autobiographical narratives on infertility, specifically memoirs, generate a counter-discourse to the stigmatising popular cultural representations of infertility. Such personal articulations, wherein authors foreground their lived experience of involuntary childlessness, not only subvert dominant stereotypes but also accord a cultural agency to the hitherto marginal perspectives on women's infertility. Additionally, the chapter recognises the cultural role of graphic memoirs on infertility in destigmatising female infertility.

Chapter 3 attempts to lay bare the ideology of pronatalism at work in the socio-cultural imaginings of motherhood, investigating the ways in which it aggravates the predicament of the childless. In close reading Paula Knight's graphic memoir, *The Facts of Life*, this chapter aims to investigate how the comics medium allows the author to arraign the ideology of pronatalism as an oppressive force that mediates her lived experience of infertility. Drawing theoretical insights from Ellen Peck, Judith Senderowitz, and Louis Althusser, among others, the chapter also seeks to investigate the socially constructed and gendered nature of motherhood as it unfolds in Knight's narrative. Finally, the chapter demonstrates how the protagonist rejects the social labelling of women based on their maternal status, and affirms her identity as an independent woman, free of the constraints of maternal ideologies.

Chapter 4 draws on the feminist critique of medicalisation to explore the misogynistic and deeply patriarchal impulses that underwrite medical attitudes towards female infertility. Further, the chapter scrutinises how infertility comics represent the medicalised female body in the clinic and the ways in which those representations foreground the dehumanising nature of the female body's medical encounter. Specifically, close reading Phoebe Potts' *Good Eggs*, Emily Steinberg's *Broken Eggs*, Paula Knight's *The Facts of Life,* and Jenell Johnson's *Present/Perfect*, the chapter demonstrates the lack of agency and autonomy that characterise the clinical experience of infertility. The chapter argues that the visual vocabulary of comics facilitates an externalisation of the psychic pain that the medical encounter engenders in the patient. Additionally, the chapter examines nuanced issues such as loss of privacy, technological intrusion, and medical apathy in the context of the infertile female body's medical encounter.

Chapter 5 investigates how the memoirists successfully navigate the affective challenges and existential dilemmas of infertility through positive coping practices. The chapter recognises the psychological concept of resilience as an adequate coping method, and close reads Paula Knight's *The Facts of Life* and Phoebe Potts' *Good Eggs* to illustrate how the authors gracefully come to terms with their infertile subjectivity. The chapter specifically foregrounds the ways in which memoirists refashion their identities and draw on their beliefs, values, and existential goals to find meaning and hope in their existence as childless women. While Potts relies on spirituality, her Jewish ancestry, and its practice of telling stories as a successful coping practice, Knight finds emotional fulfilment through alternative mothering practices such as artistic creativity and ecological consciousness. For Knight, childlessness becomes a tool for personal growth and self-discovery. Finally, the chapter affirms that the memoirists positively appraise their nonmother identity through resilient coping practices. In its totality, the book concludes that graphic memoirs on female infertility, using comics affordances, foreground the memoirists lived perspectives of childlessness with force and urgency. As such, the major goal of the book is to affirm the significance of graphic medicine as a critical space for infertile women to articulate the gendered realities of infertility in creative terms.

References

Ann, Tracy. 2019. "NIT Professor and Wife Commit Suicide over Being Childless After 10 Years of Marriage." *IDIVA*, 20 August. www.idiva.com/the-daily-agenda/indian-news/nit-professor-and-wife-commit-suicide-over-being-childless-after-10-years-of-marriage/18002197. Accessed 16 January 2021.

Balen, Frank Van, and Marcia C. Inhorn. 2002. "Introduction: Interpreting Infertility: A View from the Social Sciences." In *Infertility around the Globe: New Thinking on Childlessness, Gender, and Reproductive Technologies*, ed. M. C. Inhorn and F. Van Balen, 3–32. Berkeley: University of California Press.

Barnes, Liberty Walther. 2014. *Conceiving Masculinity: Male Infertility, Medicine, and Identity*. Philadelphia, PA: Temple University Press.

Becker, Gay, and Robert D. Nachtigall. 1992. "Eager for Medicalisation: The Social Production of Infertility as a Disease." *Sociology of Health and Illness* 14(4): 456–471. doi:10.1111/1467-9566.ep10493093.

Conrad, Peter, Thomas Mackie, and Ateev Mehrotra. 2010. "Estimating the Costs of Medicalization." *Social Science and Medicine* 70(12): 1943–1947. doi: 10.1016/j.socscimed.2010.02.019.

Czerwiec, M. K., I. Williams, S. M. Squier, M. J. Green, K. R. Myers, and S. T. Smith. 2015. *Graphic Medicine Manifesto*. University Park: Pennsylvania State University Press.

Greil, Arthur. 2002. "Infertile Bodies: Medicalization, Metaphor, and Agency." In *Infertility around the Globe: New Thinking on Childlessness, Gender, and Reproductive Technologies*, ed. M. C. Inhorn and F. Van Balen, 101–118. Berkeley: University of California Press.

Greil, Arthur, Julia Mcquillan, and Kathleen Slauson-Blevins. 2011. "The Social Construction of Infertility." *Sociology Compass* 5(8): 736–746. doi:10.1111/j.1751-9020.2011.00397.x.

Groensteen, Thierry. 2007. *The System of Comics*, tr. Bart Beaty and Nick Nguyen. Jackson: University Press of Mississippi.

Inhorn, Marcia C. 2002. "Sexuality, Masculinity, and Infertility in Egypt: Potent Troubles in Marital and Medical Encounters." *Journal of Men's Studies* 10(3): 343–359. doi:10.3149/jms.1003.343.

Jensen, Robin. 2016. *Infertility: Tracing the History of a Transformative Term*. Philadelphia: Pennsylvania University Press.

Markle, Meghan. 2020. "The Losses we Share." *New York Times*, 25 November. www.nytimes.com/2020/11/25/opinion/meghan-markle-miscarriage.html. Accessed 16 January 2021.

Mascarenhas, Maya N., Seth R. Flaxman, Ties Boerma, Sheryl Vanderpoel, and Gretchen A. Stevens. 2012. "National, Regional, and Global Trends in Infertility Prevalence since 1990: A Systematic Analysis of 277 Health Surveys." *PLoS Medicine* 9(12). doi:10.1371/journal.pmed.1001356.

May, Elaine. 1997. "The Politics of Reproduction." *Irish Journal of American Studies* 6: 1–37. www.jstor.org/stable/30003141. Accessed 20 July 2018.

McCloud, Scott. 1994. *Understanding Comics*. New York: Harper Perennial.

Nordqvist, Christian. 2018 "Infertility in Men and Women." *Medical News Today*, 4 January. www.medicalnewstoday.com/articles/165748.php. Accessed 10 October 2018.

Obama, Michelle. 2018. "'I Felt Lost and Alone': Michelle Obama Reveals Experience of Miscarriage – Video." *The Guardian*, 9 November. www.theguardian.com/us-news/video/2018/nov/09/michelle-obamamiscarriage-abc-news-interview-video-clip. Accessed 25 December 2019.

Office on Women's Health. 2017. "Infertility." www.womenshealth.gov/a-z-topics/infertility. Accessed 15 July 2019.

Patel, Ansha, P. S. V. N. Sharma, and Pratap Kumar. 2018. "'In Cycles of Dreams, Despair, and Desperation': Research Perspectives on Infertility Specific Distress in Patients Undergoing Fertility Treatments." *Journal of Human Reproductive Sciences* 11(4): 320–328. doi:10.4103/jhrs.jhrs_42_18.

Sandelowski, Margarete J. 1990. "Failures of Volition: Female Agency and Infertility in Historical Perspective." *Signs: Journal of Women in Culture and Society* 15(3): 475–499. doi:10.1086/494606.

Schmitt, Ronald. 1992. "Deconstructive Comics." *Journal of Popular Culture* 25(4): 153–162. doi:10.1111/j.0022-3840.1992.00153.x.

Squier, S. M. 2008. "Literature and Medicine, Future Tense: Making it Graphic." *Literature and Medicine* 27(2): 124–152. doi:10.1353/lm.0.0031.

Urology Care Foundation. N.d. "What is Male Infertility." www.urologyhealth.org/urologic-conditions/male-infertility. Accessed 12 October 2018.

World Health Organisation (WHO). 2009. "Infertility Definitions and Terminology." www.who.int/reproductivehealth/topics/infertility/definitions/en/. Accessed 10 October 2018.

World Health Organisation (WHO). 2012. "Global Prevalence of Infertility, Infecundity and Childlessness." www.who.int/reproductivehealth/topics/infertility/burden/en/. Accessed 11 October 2018.

1 Visualising illness
Comics and graphic medicine

Introduction

Comics and the related verbal-visual art forms such as cartoons and caricatures have a long history of engagement with healthcare and medicine. Premodern medicine has often been satirised by medical caricaturists for its archaic, inhuman, and unscientific practices. Again, significant landmarks in medicine's history, including the invention of vaccines, and the threat posed by pandemics such as cholera and Spanish flu, have been well documented in the visual canvas of artists, and such depictions also reflected the socio-political and cultural resonances of the events. Modern comics and cartoons have celebrated the advancements in healthcare and medicine, portraying healthcare professionals as heroic figures. The underground comix movement which flourished in the 1960s following comics censorship was a significant episode both in the history of comics and medicine as it foregrounded the messy and obscene aspects of corporeality, paving the way for honest depictions of illness and suffering in comics. The emergence of the graphic medicine movement in the twenty-first century is a remarkable moment in comics' engagement with healthcare and medicine as it offers a new perspective on discourses centred on health and illness. This chapter approaches graphic medicine in its generic contexts, scrutinising how this emerging discourse productively alters discourses on health and illness. The chapter delineates the ways in which comics, autobiography, and the health humanities intersect in this novel interdisciplinary field of study. The chapter contextualises the emergence of graphic medicine within health humanities and narrative medicine movements, also seeking to examine graphic pathographies as a significant addition to life narratives on illness. Specifically, the chapter discusses: the landmarks in the development of graphic medicine in relation to narrative medicine and medical/health humanities

DOI: 10.4324/9781003028628-2

movements, graphic pathographies as a subgenre of somatographies, graphic medicine and women's life writing, graphic medicine and medical pedagogy, therapeutic power of graphic pathographies, graphic medicine's role in community building, graphic medicine as a critique, and internationalisation and popularisation of graphic medicine.

Humanising healthcare: from medical humanities to health humanities

Graphic medicine's development should be understood in relation to the growth of medical humanities/health humanities in medical schools and universities. Coined by historians George Sarton and Frances Siegel in their obituary of science historian Edmund Andrews published in 1948, the term "medical humanities" refers to a multidisciplinary field that "embraces the study of medicine through the lenses of literature, history, philosophy, the social sciences, and the arts in the context of applied medicine and bioethics" (Goyette and Fairey 2020). As an approach deployed primarily in medical education and training, medical humanities seek to instil humanistic values in medical practitioners by drawing on the creative and intellectual strengths of the liberal arts. As Alan Bleakley observes, the task of medical humanities in the context of medical education involves aesthetic and political challenges. Aesthetically, medical humanities aim to transform the technical and instrumental nature of medical practice into the "art" of medicine:

> communicating sensitively with patients and colleagues; close listening in receiving the patient's history; close noticing in the physical examination; making sense of the stories that patients tell and adapting interventions accordingly; managing an identity as an expert or a connoisseur in a specialty; critically and reflexively understanding the fabric of medical culture itself; and critically and reflexively understanding historical and cultural assumptions about the body, health, disease and illness.
>
> (Bleakley 2015, 3)

Politically, medical humanities attempt the "democratizing of medicine – shifting medical practice from an authority-led hierarchy that is doctor-centred to a patient-centred and interprofessional clinical team process" (Bleakley 2015, 2). As such, medical humanities not only advocate more agency to the patients in the clinical discourse but also accentuate the need to develop empathetic values in physicians.

Historically speaking, the inclusion of humanities courses in medical curricula was part of a broader attempt to change medical education in the United States, which began with Abraham Flexner's 1910 report on medical education. Titled *Medical Education in the United States and Canada: A Report to the Carnegie Foundation for the Advancement of Teaching,* Flexner's report suggested that students with an interest to study medicine should acquire a strong foundation in sciences (Flexner 1910). The middle of the twentieth century witnessed some significant efforts to reinvent medical education. Notably, in 1937, E. E. Reinke at Vanderbilt School of Medicine emphasised the significance of "leavening technical training with a liberal education" (Bleakley and Jones 2014, 127). Subsequently, several attempts have been made to include humanities in medical education.

While Western Reserve School of Medicine in 1952 included history of medicine in its curriculum, Pennsylvania State University College of Medicine in 1967 became the first medical school to establish a humanities department, with a curriculum that "focused on engendering better understanding of families, their resources within communities, the influence of lifestyle and behaviour on the prevalence and impact of disease, and on philosophical, spiritual and ethical aspects of healthcare" (Hurwitz 2013, 673). Ever since, the growth of medical humanities in the US has been dramatic, with almost 90% of medical schools in 2011 having humanities content in their curriculum. Outside the US, the inclusion of humanities content in the medical curriculum has been slower but is steadily growing. In Canada, the University of Manitoba conducted "voluntary series of evening sessions for medical students on 'human values' in the early 1990s, which was eventually made mandatory" (Kidd and Connor 2008, 46–47). According to a 2008 survey, out of the 17 medical schools in Canada, 13 had humanities electives or some medical humanities content (Kidd and Connor 2008; Banaszek 2011). In the United Kingdom, Royal Free and the University College Medical School established its Medical Humanities Unit in 1998, and by 2018, 19 out of 33 medical schools offered medical humanities programmes (Association for Medical Humanities 2019). As of 2018, medical humanities courses are offered in medical schools in countries such as Australia, China, Germany, New Zealand, Norway, Switzerland, Singapore, and Sweden among others.

In recent years, medical humanities have evolved beyond medical schools and medical education, seen in the emergence of health humanities, a broader interdisciplinary academic field that subsumes health, medicine, and the arts. Craig Klugman defines health humanities thus:

> The health humanities [is] ... an interdisciplinary field concerned with understanding the human condition of health and illness in order to create knowledgeable and sensitive health care providers, patients, and family caregivers. As a field (meaning a focus of study rather than a disciplinary method), the health humanities draws on the methodologies of the humanities and social sciences to provide insight, understanding, and meaning to people facing illness including professional care providers, lay care providers, patients, policy-makers and others concerned with the suffering of humans.
> (Klugman 2017, 421–422)

Though related interdisciplinary approaches that link healthcare and the arts, medical humanities and health humanities differ in their focus: while medical humanities deploy humanities content as a valuable tool in medical education and practice in order to enhance the "doctoring" skills in physicians, health humanities situate "the humanities, arts, and social sciences in the centre, rather than as an add-on to clinical and basic sciences" (Klugman and Lamb 2019, 3). Put differently, "a key task of this emerging field of enquiry is to breakdown the artificial boundaries between the arts and biomedical science to identify mutually beneficial fields of study" (Crawford et al. 2015, 18).

Focusing on health, which is broader than medicine, health humanities include not only healthcare professionals and patients but also "their families, whole communities, and the fabric of our societies" (Klugman and Lamb 2019, 4) who are active agents in the experience of healing and illness. Furthermore, health humanities acknowledge the social experience of health and illness, locating health in its sociocultural environment. To quote Jones et al. (2017), "medicine is only a minor determinant of health in human populations alongside other social factors such as class, education, occupation, environment, race, and stigma" (933). As an applied enterprise, this unique interdisciplinary approach adopts diverse methodologies borrowed from multiple disciplines with a common spirit which "is not just about understanding human experience of health and healthcare; it is also about wielding a persistent voice of critique and working explicitly towards social justice" (Klugman and Lamb 2019, 4).

Several independent educational programmes on health humanities are currently conducted across universities and colleges leading to minors, certificates, master's degrees, and doctorates. Three national societies focusing on health humanities have been established worldwide: The International Health Humanities Network in the UK (2011), the Health Humanities Consortium in the US (2015), and the Canadian

Association for Health Humanities (2018). Additionally, major research bodies in the humanities such as Arts and Humanities Research Council in the UK have recognised health humanities in their programme of work, and funding bodies on healthcare research including Wellcome Trust have broadened their scope to include health humanities. In response to this gradual shift from a narrow notion of medical humanities to a broader perspective of health humanities, former centres of medical humanities are adopting more inclusive missions and nomenclatures. As Crawford et al. observe, "the genetic code of the tradition called 'medical humanities' has been radically altered by the health humanities movement and 'health humanities' looks set to become the superordinate term for the application of arts and humanities to healthcare, health and wellbeing" (Crawford 2015, 156). Interestingly, the emergence of graphic medicine as a movement and practice within academia and medical schools strengthens the medical/health humanities movements' task of "humanising" the field of healthcare and medicine in myriad ways. With a wide range of applications in interdisciplinary research and teaching in humanities, medical education, and patient care, graphic medicine offers a unique perspective to medical/health humanities.

Narrative medicine: legitimising the patient's perspective

Pioneered by physician and author Rita Charon, narrative medicine is a movement that emerged in the 1970s alongside the growth of medical humanities with the similar intention of "humanising" the field of healthcare. As a radical movement that aimed to revolutionise the practice of medicine, narrative medicine not only challenged the ideological supremacy of an authoritarian, empirical, and fact-based medical knowledge but also decried the power dichotomy in the patient–physician interactions. Defined as "clinical cousin of literature-and-medicine and a literary cousin of relationship-cantered care" (Charon 2008, vii) narrative medicine recognises the centrality of the patient's perspective and therefore accords legitimacy to the patient's experiential knowledge which was relegated to the margins by the physician's expert medical knowledge.

Foregrounding the significance of the sufferer's narrative of illness in medical practice, Charon argues thus: "I first used the phrase 'narrative medicine' in 2000 to refer to clinical practice fortified by narrative competence – the capacity to recognize, absorb, metabolize, interpret, and be moved by stories of illness" (2007, 1265). Again, while summarising the aims of narrative medicine, Lindsay Holmgren et al. underscore the significance of the physician's skill and sensitivity in analysing the patient's narrative thus:

> The goal of narrative medicine is to restore to clinicians a skill at and sensitivity to the narrative tradition that underpins all human discourse and intersubjectivities. To be sure, narrative medicine does not seek to eradicate the benefits that modern science affords medical practice. Rather, it works to understand that technology is powerless in the absence of a relationship between two human beings whose clinical encounter is both moral and instrumental.
> (2011, 255)

In sum, as an approach in medical training, narrative medicine offers "healthcare professionals with practical wisdom in comprehending what patients endure in illness and what they themselves undergo in the care of the sick" (Charon 2008, vii).

Interestingly, narrative medicine promotes the method of "attentive listening" by which the doctor listens "expertly and attentively to extraordinarily complicated narratives" of patients which are available through "words, gestures, silences, tracings, images, laboratory test results, and changes in the body" (2008, 4). Charon advocates the study of literature in narrative medicine programmes, arguing that close reading fictional representations of illness enhances physicians' "narrative competence", that is, "the ability to absorb, interpret, and respond to stories" (as quoted in Holmgren et al. 2011, 251). According to Charon, "narrative competence enables the physician to practice with empathy, reflection, professionalism, and trustworthiness, all of which together constitute narrative medicine" (Holmgren et al. 2011, 251). Today, several medical schools offer narrative medicine programmes to fortify a patient-centred treatment practice. Columbia University Medical Center launched a Master's programme in Narrative Medicine in 2009, which helps "physicians, nurses, social workers, mental health professionals, chaplains, social workers, academics, and all those interested in the intersection between narrative and medicine improve the effectiveness of care" (Columbia University Medical Center 2018).

In essence, as a holistic approach, narrative medicine aims to yoke together the scientific knowledge of the doctor and the experiential knowledge of the patient in medical practice. As an emerging interdisciplinary field, graphic medicine follows the ethos of narrative medicine in that it legitimises patients' perspective of illness, which is often relegated in medical discourse. Ian Williams in *Graphic Medicine Manifesto* emphasises this interrelationship between graphic medicine and narrative medicine thus: "graphic medicine combines the principles of narrative medicine with an exploration of the visual systems of comic art, interrogating the representation of physical and emotional signs and symptoms within the medium" (Czerwiec et al. 2015, 1). Put together, following the central tenets of narrative medicine, graphic medicine offers a creative space for patients to articulate the phenomenological and lived realities of illness and suffering, thereby according a discursive significance to their marginal perspectives.

Autopathography, graphic pathography, and life writing

Thomas Couser uses the term autopathography to signify "autobiographical narratives of illness or disability", arguing that the development of this subgenre of life writing is "a sign of cultural health – an acknowledgement and an exploration of our condition as embodied selves" (1991, 65). Couser cites the works of Robert Murphy (*The Body Silent*), Audre Lorde (*The Cancer Journals*), Oliver Sacks (*A Leg to Stand On*), and Barbara Webster (*All of a Piece: A Life with Multiple Sclerosis*) among others as examples of the burgeoning body of autopathographies. Similarly, Ann Hunsaker Hawkins employs the term "pathography" to denote "a form of autobiography or biography that describes personal experiences of illness, treatment, and sometimes death" (1999, 1). Locating the rise of pathographies in the second half of the twentieth century, Hawkins observes that this mode of life writing "embodies dynamic constructs about how to deal with disease and treatment: its images and metaphors and myths are not just decorative and fanciful but highly influential models of how to negotiate an illness experience" (1999, 11).

Later, Couser proposes the term "auto/somatography", referring to memoirs that centre on the experience of living with a "body that is usually odd or anomalous" and "living *with*, loving, or knowing intimately someone with such a body" (2009, 2). Couser deploys an alternative term "some body memoir", to distinguish auto/somatographies from "somebody memoir" (which is written by someone already famous) and from "nobody memoir" (which brings fame to an otherwise obscure writer). According to Couser, the highly touted "memoir boom" that happened in the late twentieth century is also marked by the surge of auto/somatographies, which, for him, is "a cultural and historical phenomenon of great significance" (2009, 3). Identifying the emergence of auto/somatographies on breast cancer, and AIDS as part of the rise of women's rights movements and gay rights movements, respectively, Couser recognises the political significance of such narratives. Memoirs on a wide range of other illness/disability are also identified as belonging to this subgenre: Amy Wilensky's *Passing for Normal: A Memoir of Compulsion* (OCD), Lisa Roney's *Sweet Invisible Body: Reflections on a Life with Diabetes* (diabetes), Teresa McLean's *Seized: My Life with Epilepsy* (epilepsy), Tim Brookes' *Catching My Breath: An Asthmatic Explores his Illness* (asthma), and Liane Holliday Willey's *Pretending to be Normal: Living with Asperger's Syndrome* (Asperger's syndrome) among others.

Interestingly, Michael J Green and Kimberly R Myers employ the term "graphic pathographies" to denote narratives on illness in the medium of comics or a body of "illness narratives in graphic form" which could be considered as an emerging subgenre of pathographies. Differentiating graphic pathographies from textual pathographies, Green and Myers observe thus: "[a]lthough graphic pathographies are often thematically similar to standard textual accounts of illness, their powerful visual messages convey immediate visceral understanding in ways that conventional texts cannot" (2010, 674). Close reading graphic memoirs on cancer such as Marisa Acocella Marchetto's *Cancer Vixen* and Brian Fies' *Mom's Cancer*, Green and Myers illustrate the potential of graphic pathographies to visually document autobiographical accounts of illness and suffering. In fact, there is a remarkable intersection of autopathography and graphic pathography in the emergence of autobiographical comics on illness where artists use the verbal-visual aesthetic of comics to narrativise their tribulations occasioned by illness. The genre of autobiographical comics offers a visual vocabulary for authors to document how the experience of illness alters their self-identity in diverse ways. Particularly, the comic form performs a critical role in articulating the ways in which illness produces marginal bodies and identities.

Additionally, Couser argues that graphic pathographies offer memoirists "enormous creative freedom and potential power" (2018, 4). According to Couser, by admitting "embodiment into the narrative in new ways, both literally and metaphorically" (2018, 2), graphic pathographies "fill in a lacuna that is striking even in written autosomatography: the absence of (the image of) the affected body" (2018, 3). Further, the emergence of this unique mode of narrating illness not only makes the genre of somatography accessible to authors whose preferred method of self-expression is drawing but also to a new demographic who prefers visual narrative forms over their verbal counterparts. In essence, the emergence of graphic pathographies indicates a paradigm shift in the genre of life writing in general and the subgenre of pathographies in particular, as it offers a visual-verbal vocabulary for auto/

pathographers to explore nuanced themes in relation to illness, self, and embodiment.

Comics, graphic medicine, and women's life writing

Couser theorises life writing in relation to illness and gender, arguing that "when illness strikes women, it may echo and expose the marginalization of gender" (1991, 68). Elaborating on how the growth of autopathography, as a subgenre of life writing, would enable women to articulate the gendered realities of experiencing illness, Couser observes thus:

> [i]f women and ill people are both marginalized in different ways, then sick women are doubly marginalized. With recent developments in autopathography, then, we have a return of the doubly, or perhaps triply, repressed – an overt, unembarrassed, unapologetic representation of the ill, female body.
>
> (1991, 73)

Further, discussing two women's autobiographical narratives, Barbara Webster's *All of a Piece: A Life with Multiple Sclerosis* (1989) and Nancy Mairs' *Plaintext* (1986), Couser concludes: "'ill' women may be well-equipped to reconceptualize the relation between psyche and soma, to write the life of the body as well as the life of the mind" (1991, 73). Couser's assertion that women's personal narratives on illness can illuminate the intricacies of experiencing illness in relation to gender is significant, particularly in the context of women's autopathographies. The growing body of women's autobiographical comics in which female autopathographers foreground their uniquely personal stories and visualise the gendered nature of illness experiences validates Couser's arguments.

As Hillary Chute contends, there existed a conspicuous absence of any substantive work by female artists in mainstream comics before the emergence of the comix underground in the 1960s. Accordingly, Chute emphasises the significance of the underground comix tradition in the development of women's comics in the US thus: "[i]t is only in the comics underground that the U.S. first saw any substantial work by women allowed to explore their own artistic impulses" (2010, 20). Cartoonist Trina Robbins "organized the first comic book created entirely by women", titled *It Ain't Me Babe: Women's Liberation* (1970), and hence "effectively created women's underground comics" (2010, 20). *Wimmin's Comix* (1972 to 1992) was the first female underground comic series which focused on feminist themes including homosexuality. As

Frederik Byrn Køhlert observes, the series "opened a cultural space for women to draw and publish comics" (2019, 25). The first ongoing comic book *Tits 'n' Clits* by Joyce Farmer and Lyn Chevely appeared in 1972. Notably, female comic artists who were actively involved in the underground comix movement were the pioneers in utilising the potential of autobiographical comics to explore women's health and sexuality. As Chute argues, with their unapologetic exploration of women's health and sexuality, women's underground comix illustrated "how autobiographical comics at its outset lends itself to feminist concerns about embodiment and representation" (2010, 19).

Underground artist Aline Kominsky-Crumb's "Goldie: A Neurotic Woman" (1972) is often regarded as the first female autobiographical comic to deal with the theme of women's health and sexuality. Kominsky-Crumb has inspired a host of female cartoonists of the underground movement to publish comics and cartoons on tabooed topics related to women's health such as female masturbation and menstruation. Among such narratives, Joyce Farmer and Lyn Chevli's pro-choice comic on abortion titled *Abortion Eve* (1973) holds special significance. Farmer and Chevli's text not only debates the practical challenges of unwanted pregnancies but also addresses the risks of unhygienic abortions. As Melanie McGovern and Martin Paul contend, *Abortion Eve*'s "use of the medium of the sequential narrative to relay medical information perfectly fits the criteria for a work of graphic medicine" (2019, 3) and hence is "a proto-form of contemporary graphic medicine" (2019, 4). Again, Farmer and Chevli's *Tits 'n' Clits* (1972–1987) deals with similar issues such as menstruation and birth control. *Incredible Facts O' Life Sex Education Funnies* edited by Laura Fountain was another notable visual narrative on women's health published during this period.

Inspired by the legacy of the underground comix tradition, many female artists today utilise the potential of graphic medicine not only to concretise their personal experience of illness and suffering but also to foreground the deeply gendered nature of such experiences. There is a growing body of feminist personal articulations on conditions such as breast cancer, eating disorders, and infertility, among others. Graphic memoirs on breast cancer such as Tucky Fussell's *Mammoir: A Pictorial Odyssey of the Adventures of a Fourth Grade Teacher with Breast Cancer* (2005), Marisa Acocella Marchetto's *Cancer Vixen: A True Story* (2006), Miriam Engelberg's *Cancer Made Me A Shallower Person: A Memoir* (2006), Rachel Ball's *The Inflatable Woman* (2015), Jennifer Hayden's *The Story of My Tits* (2015), and Teva Harrison's *In-Between Days* (2016) illustrate how women's experience of breast cancer is invariably mediated by cultural norms regarding feminine beauty and embodiment. These narratives also explore issues surrounding the medical experience of breast cancer, including body shaming and objectification that cause severe harm to the patients. In a similar vein, women's graphic auto/pathographies such as Nadia Shivack's *Inside Out: Portrait of an Eating Disorder* (2007), Carol Lay's *The Big Skinny: How I Changed My Fattitude* (2008), Lesley Fairfield's *Tyranny* (2009), Ludovic Debeurme's *Lucille* (2011), Karrie Fransman's *The House that Groaned* (2012), Katie Green's *Lighter than My Shadow* (2013), and Lacy J. Davis and Jim Kettner's *Ink in Water: An Illustrated Memoir (Or, How I Kicked Anorexia's Ass and Embraced Body Positivity)* (2016) portray how the mainstream culture's idealised imaginings of thin female bodies contribute to women's disordered eating. Evidently, graphic medicine is offering a visual forum for female artists to vocalise their intimate yet gendered and silenced experiences of illness with force and urgency.

Graphic medicine as a pedagogical tool

Although graphic medicine has enormous potential as a pedagogical tool, graphic pathographies need to be distinguished from educational comics disseminating health information. As interrelated subgenres of comics, both graphic medicine and educational health comics have thematic and structural overlapping. Yet graphic auto/pathographies differ significantly from comics divulging health information in terms of visual aesthetics, objectives, authorship, and reception. Produced with the aim of disseminating health information to the masses, educational health comics are linear visual-verbal narratives written in a simple form facilitating easy comprehension. On the other hand, graphic medicine narratives are mostly autobiographical accounts written by sufferers or caregivers, marked by stylistic ingenuity, thematic diversity, and formal innovations and experimentations. Apart from offering cathartic/therapeutic relief to the authors, graphic auto/pathographies aim to create awareness and form communities. While educational health comics appeal to a demographic which includes mostly sufferers and caregivers, graphic medicine appeals to a wider readership which includes not only sufferers and caregivers but also health professionals, comic enthusiasts, scholars, and the public at large. Nevertheless, graphic medicine is effectively used as a pedagogical tool, especially in medical education.

Graphic medicine narratives have been introduced in the medical curriculum in the West, especially in medical humanities/health humanities and narrative medicine programmes, with the aim of fostering doctoring skills – empathy, understanding, attentive listening, clinical reasoning, and awareness of physician bias – among medical students.

For instance, at the Penn State Milton S. Hershey Medical Center, Michael Green has launched an elective course on graphic medicine titled "Graphic Storytelling and Medical Narratives." According to Green, the course aims to achieve the following objectives:

> 1) expose students to a set of medically relevant graphic narratives that provoke critical reflection about the experience of illness and the ways patients and their families interface with the medical system; 2) equip students with critical thinking skills for reading and understanding comics that are relevant to medical practice; and 3) nurture students' creativity by helping them develop their own stories into original graphic narratives.
>
> (2013, 472)

As such, the course introduces to the fourth-year medical students graphic memoirs such as Ken Dahl's *Monsters*, Joyce Farmer's *Special Exits*, and Thom Ferrier's *Disrepute*. Students are also encouraged to make comics based on their own personal experiences.

Creating comics allows medical students "the freedom to reflect honestly (and safely) about the forces that shape their emerging professional identities" (Green 2015, 777), apart from keeping "creative skills, so critical to diagnosis and treatment, sharp" (Czerwiec et al. 2015, 154). Additionally, creating comics offers medical students a chance for self-expression, in the process, helping them develop better strategies to communicate effectively, which would also facilitate their clinical interactions. Making autobiographical comics that focus on the challenges of being a doctor can be therapeutic, especially for medical interns as it enables them to find an outlet to express their professional issues. Medical intern narratives such as Ryan Montoya's *Sign Out* and Michael Natter's *Code Blue* explore issues that the interns encounter in a highly stressful and demanding medical work environment.

Again, Czerwiec and Green contend that reading graphic narratives on illness helps healthcare professionals to critically reflect upon intricate issues impinging healthcare practices which are otherwise unacknowledged (YouTube 2013). Reading comics is an exercise that hones students' critical thinking and diagnostic skills. As Czerwiec notes elsewhere, the inherently fragmented structure of comics narrative, which requires the reader to decode, is similar to the often incoherent and fragmented structure of a patient's narrative of illness. Reading patients' personal accounts of illness also grants medical students access to the subjective and lived aspects of illness and suffering, which are often neglected in medical practice. Graphic pathographies are, hence, "a novel and creative way to learn and teach about illness ... [and] the themes and structure of this medium will resonate with an increasingly large number of medical professionals" (Green and Myers 2010, 577).

Graphic medicine as therapy, community, and critique

In *Graphic Medicine Manifesto*, Williams demonstrates how making comics and graphic medicine can be a therapeutic process that enables artists to reconstruct their identity in terms of their illness experience: "making autobiographical comics is a type of symbolic creativity that helps form identity – a way to reconstruct the world, placing fragments of testimony into a meaningful narrative and physically reconstructing the damaged body" (Czerwiec et al. 2015, 119). As Williams rightly points out, creating comics on illness and suffering not only allows the authors to creatively externalise their lived experiences but also equips them to make sense of their altered perceptions and embodied subjectivity. In order to narrativise their experience of illness, which is often incoherent and fragmented, artists usually rely on a repertoire of symbols, metaphors, and images. As such, "[t]his iconic symbolization gives experiences a visual identity because the images created contain all the elements of that experience – in other words, what happened, our emotional reactions to what happened and the horror and terror of the actual event" (Steele and Malchiodi 2012, 157). Put differently, making comics helps the subjects "to organize the emotional effects of an experience as well as the experience itself" (Pennebaker and Seagal 1999, 1249) and hence is a therapeutic activity. Notably, adopting a self-reflexive idiom, graphic medicine narratives such as David Small's *Stitches*, Katie Green's *Lighter than My Shadow*, and Phoebe Potts' *Good Eggs* illuminate how making comics and creating art allows the authors to alleviate pain and suffering that illness engenders.

The therapeutic power of graphic medicine not only lies in the process of creating comics since reading comics on illness can be cathartic and therefore, psychologically rewarding. The reader plays a crucial role in the creation of meaning in comics as the medium "offer[s] the readers the chance to actively construct, critically interpret, and consciously reflect on and relate to specific messages" (Carleton 2014, 161). Additionally, in the context of graphic medicine, reading is "an image based process of bearing witness" (Guerin and Hallas 2007, 11) where the reader not only becomes a co-creator of the meaning but also relates to the experiential realities of suffering that the author underwent. The reader gets access to the inarticulate pain and inordinate trauma that an illness engenders in the subject without literally experiencing it. Comic artist Sarah Leviatt acknowledges this healing power of graphic medicine when she recounts her experience, both as a reader and as a creator: "[g]raphic medicine has comforted and sustained me in hard times: both reading others' work and creating my own. The comics we call graphic medicine can actually act as medicine themselves – the kind of medicine that makes you feel better with no side effects" (as quoted in Czerwiec et al. 2015, 168).

Furthermore, the role of the graphic medicine movement in community building cannot be understated. To quote Squier, "community building is a central strategy of graphic medicine" (Czerwiec et al. 2015, 53). The proliferation of graphic pathographies on specific illness experiences and the emergence of various discourses centred on such narratives result in the creation of a community of sufferers, making individuals feel less alone. Creation of such communities also facilitates information sharing, mutual support, recognition, and awareness creation. Referring to her personal experience, Katie Green, for instance, affirms the empowering nature of graphic medicine communities thus: "I was met with only empathy and support. I met people from such a range of different backgrounds, many of whom became close friends and a community of support" (as quoted in Czerwiec et al. 2015, 167). Additionally, as Williams contends, graphic pathographies "offer a window into the subjective reality of other sufferers and provide companionship through a shared experience in a more immediate manner than might be gained from joining a self-help group or reading patient information leaflets" (Williams 2012, 25).

Finally, graphic medicine invests in the subversive potential of the comics medium in addressing larger socio-political and cultural concerns that impinge on healthcare and medicine. As such, graphic pathographies destabilise "the dominant methods of scholarship in healthcare, offering a more inclusive perspective of medicine, illness, disability, caregiving, and being cared for" (Czerwiec et al. 2015, 2). Arraigning biomedicine for its over-reliance on medical facts and statistical data which discount the lived and subjective nature of illness experiences, graphic memoirs inaugurate a new politics of critique, challenge, and resistance in the field of healthcare. Further, graphic memoirs on illness problematise the cartesian dualism of the biomedical paradigm that perceives the mind and the body as separate, in the process embracing a phenomenological understanding of illness as lived. Centred on the subjective experience of illness, "these stories inevitably dramatize interactions with institutional medical systems from a patient's perspective" (Pigg 2018). Many graphic memoirs on illness launch a strident critique of healthcare practices for their dominance and control over the lives of the patients, reducing them to passive subjects. Graphic pathographies such as Fies' *Mom's Cancer*, and Small's *Stitches*, for instance, illustrate the estranging nature of medical treatments. As Sarah Glazer argues, "in many of these accounts the medical establishment comes off as insensitive, incomprehensible, or dictatorial" (2015, 15). Notably, graphic medical narratives such as Peter Dunlap-Shohl's *My Degeneration: A Journey through Parkinson's* (2015) and David Wojnarowicz and James Romberge's *7 Miles a Second* (2013) address issues of inequity and inaccessibility in a bureaucratic and privatised healthcare system in the US. Again, Williams' weekly comic strip in *The Guardian* on the state of the NHS (National Health Service), titled "Sick Notes", explores, among other things, the challenges faced by the public healthcare in the UK from the economically powerful private healthcare sector. Autopathographies such as Gabby Schulz's *Sick* (2016), Emily Steinberg's *Broken Eggs* (2014), Ellen Forney's *Marbles: Mania, Depression, Michelangelo & Me* (2012), and Marisa Marchetto's *Cancer Vixen* (2009), shed light on the increasing privatisation and commoditisation of healthcare in the U.S under the neoliberal political economy of capitalism (Venkatesan and Murali 2019, n.p). These autopathographies foreground the authors' subjective experiences to critique the limits, vulnerabilities, and pitfalls of the system of healthcare, in the process pushing the contours of the personal and the political. In sum, these graphic stories "offer the social critique of the medical profession" (Green and Myers 2010, 574).

Internationalisation and popularisation of graphic medicine

Graphic medicine has acquired global recognition in the recent years through a wide variety of academic and artistic endeavours across the world. Though initially confined to the US and the UK, graphic medicine as a movement has gained popular interest and scholarly attention in Taiwan, Germany, Spain, India, Singapore, and Japan. In Taiwan, ever since the publication of Lin Tzu-Yao's *Crazy Hospital* in 2013, graphic narratives created by doctors and other healthcare professionals in Taiwanese hospitals have attained considerable popularity. At present, Taiwanese graphic medicine narratives attract a wide readership through an honest depiction of unsightly aspects of the country's healthcare in a satirical vein. As comics scholar Pin-chia Feng observes, "from the very beginning, the main purposes of Taiwanese graphic medicine are to instruct, to critique, and to entertain" (Feng 2018). The Japanese graphic medicine movement, led by Japan Graphic Medicine Association (JGMA), on the other hand, "intends to participate in the global forum of graphic medicine and communities with a focus on Japanese graphic narratives". Particularly, the association seeks to "trace a cultural history of manga and their social and cultural contributions in relation to the idea(s) of graphic medicine" (JGMA 2020).

The research project titled "PathoGraphics" (2016–2021) at Schlegel Graduate School of Literary Studies (Freie Universität Berlin, 2016) which explores English and German graphic medicine texts is a noteworthy development in Germany. The project, under the leadership of Irmela Marei Krüger-Fürhoff and Susan Merrill Squier, offers "PhD classes, public workshops, and lectures and seeks to open a dialogue with the Berlin-based comics community" (PathoGraphics website). Similarly, the School of Humanities at Nanyang Technological University, Singapore, spearheads interdisciplinary research on graphic medicine with a host of academic activities conducted annually. Led by physician and comics artist Monica Lalanda, the Spanish graphic medicine community makes significant interventions in the regionalisation of graphic medicine in Spain. Further, the Spanish website "Medicina Grafica" disseminates scholarly and artistic content for its Spanish readers. In India, even though the field is still in its infancy, an online group called "Comicos" at the University College of Medical Sciences, Delhi, deserves special mention. The brainchild of Satendra Singh, Comicos aims "to explore the impact of graphic fiction on the lives of medical professionals and patients alike" (Comicos 2020). Furthermore, the Graphic Medicine Lab at National Institute of Technology Tiruchirappalli, a scholarly group under the mentorship of Sathyaraj Venkatesan, has been conducting rigorous academic research on graphic medicine, producing a series of research articles, monographs, and dissertations.

The internationalisation of graphic medicine has also been achieved through the translation of key graphic pathographies. Brian Fies' *Mom's Cancer*, for instance, has been translated into German, French, Italian, and Japanese. Further, graphic medicine pages and groups on social media platforms including Facebook, Twitter, Instagram, and Reddit have created a global community of graphic medicine enthusiasts in the virtual space. The role of libraries in the popularisation of graphic medicine across continents cannot be overlooked. National Library of Medicine's graphic medicine project titled "Graphic Medicine: Ill-Conceived and Well Drawn!", which began in 2016 intending to popularise graphic medicine, is a must mention in this regard. Additionally, Harvard Medical School librarian Matthew Noe's weekly posts in the graphic medicine website titled "This Week in Graphic Medicine" presents graphic medicine-related events and activities around the world. Finally, the annual graphic medicine conference is an important global platform which brings together scholars, artists, and enthusiasts from across the world to deliberate upon issues centred on health and illness in comics.

Conclusion

The emergence of graphic medicine movement in the twentieth century is a remarkable moment in comics' engagement with healthcare and medicine as it offered a new perspective to discourses centred on health and illness. The ethos of graphic medicine has been inspired and shaped by the principles and practices of medical humanities/health humanities and narrative medicine movements. Taking cues from these movements, graphic medicine attempts not only to humanise healthcare and medicine but also to bring the marginalised perspectives of the patients to the centre of the medical discourse. The recent proliferation of graphic medicine narratives or graphic auto/pathographies has also enriched the field of life writing as it offers visual-verbal codes for memoirists to explore the "self" in relation to illness and suffering. Specifically, graphic medicine has enabled women to narrativise how their embodied and intimate experiences of illness have been shaped by their gender, making their identity doubly marginal. In addition to providing therapeutic/cathartic relief to pathographers, graphic medicine aims to create communities of sufferers which can make individuals feel less alone in their struggles with illness. Today, graphic medicine has attained international visibility and popularity, both as a movement and practice, owing to its widespread influence and application in discourses on healthcare and medicine.

References

Association for Medical Humanities. 2019. "UK Based Medical Humanities Programs." 8 August. https://amh.ac.uk/resources/uk-based-university-medical-humanities-provision/. Accessed 22 September 2020.
Banaszek, A. 2011. "Medical Humanities Courses Becoming Prerequisites in Many Medical Schools." *Canadian Medical Association Journal* 183(8): 441–442. doi:10.1503/cmaj.109-3830.
Bleakley, Alan. 2015. *Medical Humanities and Medical Education: How the Medical Humanities Can Shape Better Doctors*. London: Routledge.
Bleakley, Alan, and Therese Jones. 2014. *Medicine, Health and the Arts: Approaches to the Medical Humanities*. London: Routledge.

Carleton, Sean. 2014. "Drawn to Change: Comics and Critical Consciousness." *Labour/Le Travail* 73: 151–177.

Chute, Hillary L. 2010. *Graphic Women: Life Narrative and Contemporary Comics*. New York: Columbia University Press.

Columbia University Irving Medical Center. n.d. "Narrative Medicine." www.cuimc.columbia.edu/. Accessed 15 August 2018.

Comicos. 2020. "COMICOS Graphic Medicine Club of Medical Humanities Group, U.C.M.S: About." http://comicos-graphicmedicineclub-ucms.blogspot.com/p/about.html. Accessed 10 October 2020.

Couser, G. Thomas. 1991. "Autopathography: Women, Illness, and Lifewriting." *Illness, Disability, and Lifewriting* 6(1): 65–75. doi:10.1080/08989575.1991.10814989.

Couser, G. Thomas. 2009. *Signifying Bodies: Disability in Contemporary Life Writing*. Ann Arbor: University of Michigan Press.

Couser, G. Thomas. 2018. "Is there a Body in This Text? Embodiment in Graphic Somatography." *A/b: Auto/Biography Studies* 33(2): 1–27. doi:10.1080/08989575.2018.1445585.

Crawford, Paul, Brian Brown, Charley Baker, Victoria Tischler, and Brian Abrams. 2015. *Health Humanities*. London: Palgrave Macmillan.

Charon, Rita. 2007. "What to Do with Stories: The Sciences of Narrative Medicine." *Canadian Family Physician* 53(8): 1265–1267.

Charon, Rita. 2008. *Narrative Medicine: Honouring the Stories of Illness*. Oxford: Oxford University Press.

Czerwiec, M.K., Ian Williams, Susan Merrill Squier, Michael J. Green, Kimberly R. Myers, and Scott Thompson Smith. 2015. *Graphic Medicine Manifesto*. University Park: Pennsylvania State University Press.

Feng, Pin-chia. 2018. "Listen to the Doctors: Graphic Medicine in Taiwan." www.graphicmedicine.org/listen-to-the-doctors-graphic-medicine-in-taiwan/. Accessed November 2020.

Flexner, Abraham. 1910. *Medical Education in the United States and Canada: A Report to the Carnegie Foundation for the Advancement of Teaching*. New York: Carnegie Foundation for the Advancement of Teaching.

Freie Universität Berlin. 2016. "PathoGraphics: About the Project." www.geisteswissenschaften.fu-berlin.de/friedrichschlegel/assoziierte_projekte/Pathographics/sl_2_ABOUT/index.html. Accessed 10 October 2020.

Glazer, Sarah. 2015. "Graphic Medicine: Comics Turn a Critical Eye on Health Care." *Hastings Center Report* 45(3): 15–19.

Goyette, Michael, and Emily Fairey. 2020 "CLAS 3239 | Ancient Medicine: The Classical Roots of the Medical Humanities." Brooklyn College Library LibGuides Home at Brooklyn College Library. 31 January. https://libguides.brooklyn.cuny.edu/ancientmedicine_goyette/home. Accessed 17 December 2020.

Green, Michael J. 2013. "Teaching with Comics: A Course for Fourth-Year Medical Students." *Journal of Medical Humanities* 34(4): 471–476. doi:10.1007/s10912-013-9245-5.

Green, Michael J. 2015. "Comics and Medicine." *Academic Medicine* 90(6): 774–779. doi:10.1097/acm.0000000000000703.
Green, Michael J., and Kimberly R. Myers. 2010. "Graphic Medicine: Use of Comics in Medical Education and Patient Care." *BMJ (Clinical Research Ed.)* 340: 574–577. doi:10.1136/bmj.c863.
Guerin, Frances, and Roger Hallas. 2007. *The Image and the Witness: Trauma, Memory and Visual Culture*. New York: Wallflower Press.
Hawkins, Anne Hunsaker. 1999. *Reconstructing Illness: Studies in Pathography*. West Lafayette, IN: Purdue University Press.
Holmgren, Lindsay, Abraham Fuks, Donald Boudreau, Tabitha Sparks, and Martin Kreiswirth. 2011. "Terminology and Praxis: Clarifying the Scope of Narrative in Medicine." *Literature and Medicine* 29(2): 246–273. doi:10.1353/lm.2011.0323.
Hurwitz, Brian. 2013. "Medical humanities: Lineage, excursionary sketch and rationale." *Journal of Medical Ethics* 39(11): 672–674. doi: 10.1136/medethics-2013-101815
Japan Graphic Medicine Association (JGMA). 2020. "About: Our Vision." https://graphicmedicine.jp/about-en/. Accessed 10 October 2020.
Jones, Therese, Michael Blackie, Rebecca Garden, and Delese Wear. 2017. "The Almost Right Word: The Move from Medical to Health Humanities." *Academic Medicine* 92(7): 932–935. doi:10.1097/acm.0000000000001518.
Kidd, M. G., and J. T. H. Connor. 2008. "Striving to Do Good Things: Teaching Humanities in Canadian Medical Schools." *Journal of Medical Humanities* 29(1): 45–54. doi:10.1007/s10912-007-9049-6.
Klugman, Craig M. 2017. "How Health Humanities Will Save the Life of the Humanities." *Journal of Medical Humanities* 38(4): 419–430.
Klugman, Craig M., and Erin Gentry Lamb. 2019. *Research Methods in Health Humanities*. New York: Oxford University Press.
Køhlert, Byrn Frederik. 2019. *Serial Selves: Identity and Representation in Autobiographical Comics*. New Brunswick, NJ: Rutgers University Press.
Mcgovern, Melanie, and Martin Paul Eve. 2019. "Information Labour and Shame in Farmer and Chevli's Abortion Eve." *The Comics Grid: Journal of Comics Scholarship* 9(1): 1–28. doi:10.16995/cg.158.
Pennebaker, James W., and Janel D. Seagal. 1999. "Forming a Story: The Health Benefits of Narrative." *Journal of Clinical Psychology* 55(10): 1243–1254. doi:10.1002/(sici)1097-4679(199910)55:10<1243::aid-jclp6>3.0.co;2-n.
Pigg, Stacy Leigh. 2018. "Things Anthropologists Can Do with Comics." *Medical Anthropology Quarterly* 32(1). http://medanthroquarterly.org/2018/03/19/things-anthropologists-can-do-withcomics/. Accessed 5 April 2018.
Steele, William, and Cathy A. Malchiodi. 2012. *Trauma-Informed Practices with Children and Adolescents*. New York: Routledge.
Venkatesan, Sathyaraj, and Chinmay Murali. 2019. "Graphic Medicine and the Critique of Contemporary U.S. Healthcare." *Journal of Medical Humanities*, 16 August. doi: 10.1007/s10912-019-09571-z.

Williams, Ian C. M. 2012. "Graphic Medicine: Comics as Medical Narrative." *Medical Humanities* 38(1): 21–27. doi:10.1136/medhum-2011-010093.

YouTube. 2013. "Mayo Clinic Transform 2013 Symposium, 'INSIGHTS' with MK Czerwiec and Michael Green, M.D." *Mayo Clinic,* 17 October. www.youtube.com/watch?v=zTRvoQGBs0Y. Accessed 30 November 2020.

2 Imagining "the barren"
Cultural representations of women's infertility

Introduction

The biocultural perspective of illness accentuates the centrality of culture in mediating the lived realities of the sufferers. As such, the experience of illness is not shaped by biomedical aspects alone since cultural factors are decisive in determining the social meanings of disease and suffering. Representations of illness in various cultural artifacts (re)shape the collective perceptions towards different disease conditions. Popular cultural media such as films, novels, television programmes, and advertisements generate cultural ideologies which inform public attitudes towards the ill. Arguably, popular cultural texts often perpetuate stereotypical and normative conceptualisations of illness, which impact the afflicted negatively. Taking these cues, the present chapter explores the popular cultural representations of women's infertility, illustrating how such imaginings reinforce dominant stereotypes and erroneous perceptions surrounding the problem. Examining diverse popular cultural texts, spread across various media and genres such as women's magazines, novels, advertisements, TV melodramas, horror films, and reality TV shows, the chapter lays bare the politics of representation in the context of female infertility. Finally, the chapter demonstrates how women's autobiographical narratives on infertility, specifically memoirs, generate a counter-discourse to the stigmatising popular cultural representations of infertility. Such personal articulations, wherein authors foreground their lived experience of involuntary childlessness, not only subvert dominant stereotypes but also accord a cultural agency to the hitherto marginal perspectives on women's infertility.

DOI: 10.4324/9781003028628-3

Illness and representations

> An awareness of the role that culture plays in the experience of illness unavoidably invokes questions and texts lying far outside the ordinary range of medical knowledge. We must explore, for example, not only laboratory data and epidemiological research but also novels, television programs, films, [and] advertising ... The disparate texts and activities that represent the domain of culture cannot be off-limits to a study of postmodern illness.
>
> (David B. Morris 1998, 43)

> [T]he pictures or representations of bodies that we conjure up in our minds influences our experience of the real bodies (including our own) that we come upon in life. One of the cornerstones of the humanities is that the study of the body, its processes and illnesses, is pervasively affected by our own cultural presuppositions about bodies.
>
> (Sander L. Gilman 2014, 171)

David Morris, in his theorisation of the postmodern biocultural model of illness, affirms a "prominent place to the idea of culture" (Morris 1998, 41). Illness, according to Morris, is "always created at the crossroads of biology and culture," and hence should be perceived "not as the malfunctioning of a biophysical mechanism but as the unique experience of a meaning-making and embodied cultural being" (Morris 2000, 8). Morris' assertion recognises the role of cultural codes and discourses in mediating the experience of health and illness. Cultural representations are crucial in creating the social meanings of illness by both reflecting and (re)shaping public perceptions and attitudes towards illness conditions. At another level, the sufferers often internalise such imaginings of illness produced and disseminated through various cultural texts and artefacts. As Sander Gilman in his *Disease and Representation: Images of Illness from Madness to AIDS* contends, culturally produced images of illness and the ill not only influence public attitudes but also the suffering subject's perception of the self (Gilman 1988, 2). Among representations, the influential role of popular cultural texts such as films, fictions, TV programmes, and advertisements in shaping collective meanings of illness cannot be understated. These popular cultural media are powerful agents in moulding the public perceptions of illness and those who suffer from it because they are not just "a reflection of the world," but rather "an active, if not the primary, shaper of reality" (Jenkins et al. 2002, 39).

Imagining "the barren" 37

Put differently, popular culture produces, in the context of illness, what Stuart Hall defines as cultural ideology: "those images, concepts and premises which provide the frameworks through which we represent, interpret, understand and 'make sense' of some aspect of social existence" (Hall 1995, 18).

An examination of popular cultural representations of illness reveals that such depictions, intentionally or inadvertently, often create and reinforce negative stereotypes concerning illness conditions and sufferers. To quote Deborah Lupton, popular culture's "representations of the ill body are inherently political, seeking to categorize and control deviancy, [and] valorize normality" (Lupton 2003, 83). Essentialising and stereotyping portrayals of illness conditions pervade popular cultural imagery. Particularly, popular culture has a long history of misrepresenting diseases such as plague, cancer, AIDS, schizophrenia, bipolar disorder, and Alzheimer's. Susan Sontag in her seminal works *Illness as Metaphor* (1978) and *AIDS and Its Metaphors* (1989) demonstrates how, along with other cultural artefacts, popular cultural texts such as novels and films perpetuate demoralising metaphors of illness which affect the afflicted adversely. As Sontag argues, while plagues are "invariably regarded as judgements on society," both AIDS and cancer are represented as divine punishments, and results of an unhealthy lifestyle, addiction, and self-indulgence (Sontag 1989, 113). Speaking in the context of cancer, Sontag notes the adverse impact of such restrictive cultural imaginings of illness on the victims: "[a]s long as a particular disease is treated as an evil, invincible predator, not just a disease, most people with cancer will indeed be demoralized by learning what disease they have" (7).

Again, analysing popular Hollywood film representations of AIDS in the 1980s reveals how popular culture was instrumental in framing sexual minorities as the causal agent of the contagion. To quote Emma Gray Munthe, "[t]he early story of AIDS was all about 'family values', homophobia, stereotyping and fear of the other" (Munthe 2020). Malynnda A. Johnson's examination of popular TV dramas' portrayal of HIV/AIDS illustrates that the popular cultural landscape of AIDS representations continues to be erroneous and steeped in stereotypes. Johnson argues:

> [t]hree decades have come and gone since HIV and AIDS were identified; yet, … the stigma and misperceptions surrounding it remain. Stereotypes still plague HIV narratives and there continues to be an absence of voice for those who live with HIV and AIDS.
> (Johnson 2013, 1138)

38 Imagining "the barren"

Popular imaginings of mental illness conditions are no less misleading and stigmatising. As Susan M. Behuniak in her article "The Living Dead? The Construction of People with Alzheimer's Disease as Zombies" contends, the zombie imagery permeates the popular cultural figurations of the disease, "constructing them as animated corpses and their disease as a terrifying threat to the social order" (Behuniak 2011, 72). In popular narratives, patients with Alzheimer's are also portrayed as senile and abject individuals. Films and popular TV shows such as *Halloween* (1978), *Fatal Attraction* (1987), *Mr Jones* (1993), *Degrassi* (2001–2015), *Homeland* (2011–2020), and *Empire* (2015–2020) include unflattering stereotypes about the mentally ill as violent and murderous. Such distorted images of the insane "overtly or covertly colour our concept and serve to categorize them upon first glance" (Gilman 1982, iii).

Arguably, popular culture's essentialising portrayals of the sick is most evident while representing women's illness conditions. Investigating the popular cultural representations of women's illness conditions highlights the role of gender in the way mainstream cultural codes and ideologies inform representations of ill bodies. Fosket et al., for instance, in their analysis of popular media representations of breast cancer, argue thus: "media messages effectively shift our focus away from larger social, environmental, political, and economic issues surrounding breast cancer and, instead, blame individual women for their illness" (Fosket et al. 2000, 304). Put differently, such popular narratives incorrectly hold women responsible for the condition, very often leading to stigmatisation and psychic violence on the sufferers. In this context, an examination of popular cultural representations of women's infertility can reveal how popular texts create and contribute to the cultural derision and stigmatisation of women's infertility, causing irreparable social and psychological damage to the sufferers.

Infertile women in popular novels and mass-market women's magazines

Cultural historian Tracey Loughran, in her examination of the portrayal of female infertility in British mass-market women's magazines published between the 1960s and 1980s, criticises these politically and socially conservative popular texts for "valorizing motherhood and promoting a narrow and oppressive conceptualization of femininity" (Loughran 2017, 432). Eulogising maternal devotion as "love in its purest and most passionate form" (*Woman's Own* 1962, 16), women's magazines "consistently represented infertile women as desperate and tragic," and their childlessness was treated as both personal and social loss (Loughran 2017, 438). In fact, such a narrow perspective suited magazines' and the dominant culture's idea of motherhood as women's natural and therefore most fulfilling personal and social role (Loughran 2017, 436). Additionally, medical counsels given by magazines' experts to infertile women were characterised by a lack of faith in reproductive medicine, and such advice often asked women to come to terms with this "punishing hand of faith" (Proops 1967, n.p). Evident here are the essentialising, stereotyping, and scientifically erroneous portrayals of female infertility and maternity. Put together, mass-market women's magazines are guilty of unleashing social and epistemic violence on childless women.

While Loughran's critique of women's magazines offers valuable historical insights about the cultural politics surrounding infertility, contemporary fictional narratives, particularly novels, illustrate the callous portrayal of infertility issues in popular texts today. Robin Ganev, for instance, cites David Bergen's *Stranger* (2015) and Margaret Atwood's *Handmaid's Tale* (1985), and laments that "even our most celebrated authors" propagate "the myth that women who can't conceive bear some moral failing" (Ganev 2017). In the *Stranger*, for instance, the protagonist Iso, a Guatemalan woman who works in a fertility clinic, was robbed of her child by Susan, an infertile American woman. Through Iso's perspective, Bergen's novel not only pictures Susan as a child snatcher but also as an evil, empty, and ignorant woman. Iso comments about Susan's character thus: "like all the other women I've treated. She's spoiled. She's sad. She's full of want. She's greedy. She sees only herself" (quoted in Ganev 2017). According to Ganev, "*Stranger* echoes some of the stereotypes of Margaret Atwood's *A Handmaid's Tale*," since in both the texts "a woman's happiness is contingent on the creation of a child" (Ganev 2017). Atwood's story conflates sexuality and fertility in representing the fertile Handmaid as sexually attractive while infertile Serena as "withered" and "stale," and hence, no longer sexually appealing (Ganev 2017). Interestingly, Atwood's conflation of sexuality and fertility in the context of childlessness finds parallels in yet another popular text, P. D. James' dystopian novel *The Children of Men* (1992), which imagines humanity suffering from mass infertility. James' narrator, Theodore Faron, not only attributes the cause of his community's infertile predicament to the contemporary crisis of sexual values and practices but also perceives sexual intercourse without procreation as a "meaningless acrobatic" (James 1994, 167). Similarly, Sinéad Moriarty's trilogy of novels, *The Baby Trail* (2004), *A Perfect Match* (2005), and *From Here to Maternity* (2006) which explore various facets of motherhood, descends into stereotypes when presenting issues related to infertility. The book series which centres on Emma Hamilton's trials and tribulations of navigating infertility and adoption often resort to an unrealistic depiction of the subject which alienates infertile readers. Yet the trilogy has achieved tremendous popularity, with *The Baby Trail* translated into 25 languages (Shigley 2017, 49). Arguably, most popular novels, like other major popular cultural texts, are rife with negative stereotypes about women's infertility.

Self-blame and neurosis in TV melodramas

As a form of popular culture that creates an immediate emotional connection with the audience, melodramas have a crucial role in mediating the cultural conversations surrounding women's infertility. To quote Brooke Edge, "melodrama – marked by [an] excess of emotions and often gendered as feminine – is a source for representations of infertile women, and an important popular culture mode for analysing cultural anxieties around infertility" (Edge 2015, 66). While infertility appears in contemporary melodramatic films and television texts as a recurring theme, such "representations ultimately adhere to prevailing pronatalist, [and] patriarchal ideology" (Edge 2015, 67). An examination of modern American TV series such as *Grey's Anatomy*, its spin-off *Private Practice,* and *Sex and the City* reveals how popular melodramas in the West reinscribe the socio-culturally laden stereotypes surrounding childlessness. Alternatively, Bollywood melodramas such as *Chori Chori Chupke Chupke* (2001), which has generated controversy by drawing an analogy between surrogacy and prostitution, illustrate pop culture's perpetuation of negative stereotypes about infertility and related issues in non-western cultures.

In *Grey's Anatomy*, the themes of infertility and pregnancy loss find multiple iteration as characters encounter trouble conceiving and staying pregnant. Meredith Grey, the titular character who is a professionally accomplished surgeon, undergoes a miscarriage and suffers from infertility. Grey refers to herself as "barren" with a "hostile" uterus and is depicted as deeply emotional and frustrated. The protagonist decides to end her infertility treatments when the side effects of "baby drugs" impede her professional responsibilities (Allen 2011). Finally, Grey adopts a baby to fulfil her maternal aspirations. Apart from Grey, another main character Addison Montgomery is diagnosed as having "no fertility potential" by a fertility expert. Montgomery laments that she did not try to conceive a child because of her prioritisation of career over childbearing. The character dismisses a man who shows interest in her thus: "I am out of time. I missed my chance … I'm all barren. And dried up" (Grossman 2007). Elsewhere, Montgomery links her professional achievements with her infertile predicament: "apparently, as a successful woman in her 30s I don't deserve to have children" (quoted in Misiano 2007).

Montgomery is the lead character in *Private Practice,* and the series portrays how the surgeon gradually blames herself for her infertility and grows bitter over her accomplishments:

> It's not that I didn't want kids. It's because I took having kids for granted. Because a 13-year-old girl can do it. Because a 75-year-old man can do it! You know who can't do it? An overeducated, talented, strong, powerful woman in her 40s.
> (quoted in Gaviola 2011)

Throughout the series, Montgomery is depicted as desperately attempting to get pregnant, including by two failed IVFs. While undergoing IVF, the character is represented as emotionally unstable, crying, fainting, screaming, and threatening to hurt others. Just like Grey's, Montgomery's infertility struggles culminate in adopting a baby. Eventually, Montgomery conceives after her adoption. In a similar fashion, *Sex and the City* features one of the lead characters Charlotte suffering from infertility, when she marries in season three. Charlotte's first marriage crumbles partly owing to the couple's infertility, and the character undergoes a miscarriage and several infertility treatments. Charlotte is depicted as emotionally vulnerable, shouting at strangers, and often behaving neurotically in her pursuit of motherhood. The emotional impact of infertility manifests in Charlotte to the extent that she withdraws from social life and alienates friends and her (first) husband. Finally, Charlotte and her second husband choose adoption as a path towards their parenthood, and Charlotte becomes pregnant post-adoption.

These melodramatic narratives reinforce multiple stereotypes and false assumptions concerning infertility. The portrayal of Montgomery and Charlotte's pregnancy after adoption, for instance, is "emblematic of long standing (but scientifically unfounded) beliefs that infertile couples who adopt are more likely to subsequently conceive naturally" (Edge 2015, 89). This depiction contributes to what Marsh and Romer identify as a rise in media coverage of infertility which implies adoption as a cure for infertility (Marsh and Romer 1996, 168–169). To quote Edge, "post-adoption surprise pregnancies in popular culture, help bolster the presumed psychological unsuitability to mother as an underlying factor behind infertility" (Edge 2015, 89). Again, these texts depict infertile women as excessively emotional neurotics, and thus reinforce the assumption that childless women are "somehow disordered in both mind and body" (Edge 2015, 94). At another level, when Montgomery blames herself and her career accomplishments for her infertile predicament, the narrative reinforces the deep-seated patriarchal sentiment that women's education and career are an obstacle to her maternal role. The series improvises a gendered perspective of infertility as a disorder caused by women's behavioural or psychological faults. In sum, these melodramatic narratives reinscribe the inherently gendered and marginalising mainstream perspectives on female infertility in emotional terms.

Egg-freezing ads and the rhetoric of choice

The idealisation of women's maternal identity is a dominant theme that often pervades gender advertisements,[1] and they shape and perpetuate socially condoned "ideologies of motherhood and mothering practices" (Lynch 2005, 35). Maternity is framed in most gender ads as an identity that every woman should strive for, and hence, non-mothers, including infertile women, are not only stigmatised but also symbolically placed outside the normative standards of true womanhood. The recent proliferation of ads by fertility clinics and parenting companies which celebrate maternity, and unapologetically pathologise women's non-mother identity underscores this reality. These ads are illustrative of the misogynistic and stigmatising way in which women's infertility is constructed in advertisements.

An audio-visual advertisement titled "Extend Fertility: It's Your Life and Plan" which promotes the New York-based fertility clinic Extend Fertility's egg-freezing[2] treatment begins with a voice-over: "when it comes to a woman's life, there seems to be some sort of a plan already in place. It's like someone says go, and we are expected to get our decks in a row for the ultimate event, having a baby" (YouTube 2016). The ad suggests that achieving pregnancy is a difficult task for women after their early thirties, and therefore, those who delay their pregnancy prioritising their education and career might end up childless. Projecting Extend Family's egg-freezing service as a solution to such a crisis, the ad claims that a 40-year-old woman can have a baby using eggs which were collected and frozen when she was a "twenty-seven-year-old spring chicken" (YouTube 2016). Evidently, the ad recognises "how women's lives are popularly conceived – that there is [a] plan already in place of all the things you need to get done" (Harvey 2019), with the ultimate event in her life being having a baby. Further, the ad "problematically

Imagining "the barren" 43

reinforces a culturally sanctioned, idealised maternal femininity which is based on the pernicious myth that today's women can 'have it all'" (Williamson 2019). Furthermore, the advertisers not only present reproductive technologies as a solution to modern women's infertility but also construct a non-mother identity as unacceptable. In constructing infertility as easily avoidable through egg freezing and similar advanced reproductive techniques, the ad holds women responsible for their childlessness. As Williamson notes, the ad implicitly suggests that "blame can be apportioned to the infertile individual woman, who is haunted now not only by her own loss and grief, but also the spectre of failure" (Williamson 2019). The ad not only conflates maternity and femininity but also castigates infertile women by blaming them for their condition through the neoliberal rhetoric of choice. In sum, Extend Fertility's egg-freezing ad is one such instance where advertisements, as a popular cultural form, perpetuate false and misleading assumptions regarding infertility.

Infertile monsters in reality TV, and horror films

There exists a growing corpus of reality TV shows that focus on and feature real-life stories of infertile women. An examination of infertility reality TV shows[3] reveals that such shows persistently attribute "abnormal" or monstrous qualities to infertile women. Put differently, infertile women are represented in these shows as figurations of monstrosity. In their analysis of seven infertility reality TV shows, Boer et al. identify four types of monstrosity attributed to infertile women: "the cyborg, the freak, the abject, and the childless" (Boer et al. 2019). These monstrous figurations of infertility, the authors argue, "involve mechanisms of altering, excluding, or condemning infertility in relation to what is considered normal and acceptable womanhood" (Boer et al. 2019). As the female protagonists in these shows extensively engage with a wide variety of medical technologies, tools, and artefacts, they are stereotypically depicted as human-technology hybrids/infertile cyborgs. Shows such as *Rattled, Kate & Jon Plus 8,* and *A Baby Story* borrow the monstrous figure of the freak to depict women who end up with multiple pregnancy following infertility treatment. These shows also blame women for their odd choices, lifestyles, and bodies and stress the need to self-discipline in order to achieve a successful pregnancy (Boer et al. 2019).

Apart from the cyborg and the freak, the infertility reality shows represent another monstrous figure, the abject woman, which is invisible yet present. These shows always present women with "clean, unblemished bodies and perfectly make-uped faces," and this absence of abject visuals carry moral and social connotations. As such, reality TV reinforces the perception that women should "discipline and perfect their bodies to proper ones during infertility treatment, thereby securing the order of the proper" (Boer et al. n.p). The last category of monstrosity that pervades infertility reality shows is the "childless woman" who very much like the "abject woman" is made ostensibly absent in these shows. Predominantly, reality shows portray women who, after/during infertility treatment, attain motherhood, making those who remain childless invisible. Shows such as *A Conception Story* and *The Little Couple* in which the protagonists fail to achieve a successful pregnancy depict women choosing adoption as a path towards their maternal identity. Essentially, in these shows, "having a baby is explicitly or implicitly depicted as diminishing or even overcoming one's monstrosity" (Boer et al. 2019, n.p).

In a similar vein, analysing the representation of infertility as a monstrous condition in horror films, Edge observes, "infertile women who exist outside social normality of their sex and the motherhood mandate are demonized in an effort to do away with a perceived social threat" (2015, 107). Furthermore, when childless women give birth through medical assistance, their inherent monstrosity is "passed down to the resulting monstrous children" (2015, 102). Such narratives frame infertile women as an abject category: "an infertile woman is never fertile, even if she has children with medical intervention or adoption. She still cannot conceive 'naturally.' This abjection of infertile women makes them monstrous and unfit to be mothers. Any children they might have, then, are improper and aberrant, carrying monstrosity as an inherited trait" (Edge 2015, 115). Horror movies such as *It's Alive* (1974) and *Grace* (2009) reinforce such appallingly outrageous imaginings of infertility as monstrosity. Paul Solet's *Grace* centres on the monstrous mother Madeline who conceives after three years of struggles with infertility and miscarriage and decides to give birth to her child, who according to her doctors, was already dead. Madeline delivers a monstrous girl, Grace, who craves blood and sucks her mother's blood. Larry Cohen's *It's Alive*, on the other hand, features a mutant baby with fangs and claws who, upon delivery, not only kills the nurses and doctors but also slays many others before being finally shot by the police. Questioned by the police, the killer baby's mother Lenore Davis suggests that she took fertility drugs to conceive the child since she "wanted him too much" (Edge 2015, 118). The infertile heroine in Ridley Scott's *Prometheus* (2012) also creates a monstrous foetus after her husband cures her infertility by injecting an alien substance. The attribution of monstrosity to women's infertility by reality TV shows and horror movies attains significance because the cultural mainstream has "always considered anything that opposes or lies outside the ideological status quo as intrinsically monstrous and unnatural" (Benshoff 1997, 12). As such, the popular culture's invocation of the monster and the monstrous while representing women's infertility demonstrates how childless women become a deviant and unnatural category in the sociocultural mainstream.

Countering infertile subjectivity in women's memoirs

Unlike most of the mainstream cinematic representations, Hollywood film *Private Life* (2018), written and directed by Tamara Jenkins, contains a nuanced and non-stereotypical portrayal of female infertility. The film revolves around the middle-aged couple Richard (a former theatre director) and Rachel (a writer) as they embark on a desperate and difficult mission to conceive a child. Opening with a visual of Richard administering a shot to Rachel's backside, *Private Life* documents the couple's (especially Rachel's) physical and emotional trials to become parents. From undergoing medical procedures including IUI, IVF, and donor egg treatment to trying to adopt a child, Richard and Rachel pursue every available option, enduring pain, humiliation, and self-loathing in the process. Furthermore, the film explores issues such as the unethical practices in the fertility industry, and the existential dilemmas of women when they are forced to choose between career and motherhood. Although the couple fails in their many attempts at parenthood, the movie ends on a note of mutual love and hopeful optimism when Richard reassuringly holds Rachel's hands and waits for the woman who has expressed interest in them being her child's potential parents. As David Sims rightly observes, Jenkins' fertility comedy is "funny, mournful, and human, all at once" (Sims 2018), offering a nuanced and complex depiction of female infertility and its myriad dimensions.

Presumably, *Private Life* differs from other popular visual narratives in its rendition of infertility primarily because Jenkins herself has been struggling with infertility. Cath Clarke underscores the significance of this autobiographical element in *Private Life* thus: "[s]he [Jenkins] wrote the script after undergoing fertility treatment and the detail is brutally accurate" (Clarke 2018). Elsewhere, Jenkins comments on the autobiographical nature of *Private Life* thus: "the launch pad was my own experience because I and my husband went through a lot of – we tried to adopt, we tried a lot of things like that" (as quoted in Tenreyro 2018).

The autobiographical nature of Jenkins' film which offers a realistic portrayal of infertility attests to the significance of personal narratives which provide a nuanced and non-stereotypical representation of infertility. Arguably, such stories can counteract and challenge existing stereotypes and regressive perceptions of childlessness in the cultural mainstream. In this context, a growing corpus of women's memoirs in which the authors realistically portray their lived realities of infertility attains significance. Memoirs such as Paulette Alden's *Crossing the Moon: A Journey through Infertility* (1996), Anitha Jayadevan's *Malicious Medicine: My Experience with Fraud and Falsehood in* Infertility Clinics (2009), Anne-Marie Scully's *Motherhoodwinked: An Infertility Memoir* (2014), Belle Boggs' *The Art of Waiting: On Fertility, Medicine, and Motherhood* (2016), Elizabeth Katkin's *Conceivability: What I Learned Exploring the Frontiers of Fertility* (2018), and Callie Micks' *The Baby Binder: How Unexplained Infertility Forced me to Take Charge of my Life, Health and Medical Treatment so that I Could Live Better and Make Babies* (2018) explore the fraught contours of infertility through the authors' lived perspectives.

Arguably, these women's memoirs on infertility offer a counter-narrative to the stereotypical and marginalising representations of infertility in popular culture by foregrounding the authors' lived and subjective realities. Developing a counter-discourse to dominant and popular narratives of infertility which stigmatise the condition, women's infertility memoirs foreground what Elizabeth Wilson identifies as the liberative potential of life writing as a feminist literary genre: "if there is a typical literary form of feminism it is the fragmented, intimate form of confessional, personal testimony, autobiography, the diary, 'telling it like it was'" (quoted in Loughran 2017, 451). Delineating the authors' trials and tribulations of experiencing infertility, these memoirs offer valuable insights about the physical, psychological, medical, and cultural aspects of women's childlessness. In *Crossing the Moon*, Alden not only recounts her long and painful period of mourning and coping with infertility but also affirms how writing, along with the support of the family and other childless women, enabled her to overcome the grief, and to enjoy and appreciate life without children. Boggs' *The Art of Waiting*, on the other hand, offers diverse perspectives on infertility, ranging from tracing the depiction of infertility in literature and film to reporting the experiences and reflections of those who navigated the crisis of involuntary childlessness. Additionally, Boggs documents the works of self-help groups, global online infertility communities, and organisations such as RESOLVE[4] in alleviating the pain of infertile women. Unlike most infertility memoirs, Jayadevan's *Malicious Medicine* depicts the experience of infertility in a non-western cultural environment. The narrative is a horrifying account of the author's experience of malpractice in an infertility clinic in India. Jayadevan painfully recounts eight harrowing years of her life undergoing treatment for infertility and the hurt and violence such an experience engendered in her. Citing her personal experience, Jayadevan launches a staunch critique of infertility care in India, which was expensive and invasive for her. The memoir delineates Jayadevan's physical ordeals and psychological trauma while receiving treatment from callous, inefficient, and unfeeling medical practitioners. The memoir concludes with the author's plea for a code of law in India to regulate ART treatments so that other women are spared from the anguish and malpractice that she experienced.

As the title indicates, Scully's *Motherhoodwinked* documents the author's frustration and sense of betrayal after the realisation that motherhood was not a given, as she was made to believe since her childhood. The memoir depicts the author navigating through her complex pregnancy plan and a host of medical procedures with the hope of overcoming her infertility. At another level, *Motherhoodwinked* is a social commentary on the impact of infertility on the sufferers and the role of the society in the modern digital age in both alleviating and aggravating their suffering. As such, the memoir offers coping strategies for those who go through infertility and its attendant socio-cultural challenges. Finally, Katkin's *Conceivability* and Micks' *The Baby Binder*, the two memoirs published in 2018, are armed with a wealth of information on fertility science that the authors have gained through their personal experiences. While Katkin's attempts to seek answers for her unexplained infertility enables her to present a comprehensive account of infertility treatments around the globe, Micks' narrative laments the insensitive public responses to women's reproductive failures. Cumulatively, these women's memoirs, with a nuanced and subjective representation of infertility, perform a cultural work of removing the myths and stigma surrounding involuntary childlessness and related reproductive disorders in women. In so doing, these personal renditions of infertility become what Thomas Couser terms as "quality of life writing"[5]: the body of life narratives which has a "great potential to demystify and destigmatise the conditions it recounts from the inside" (Couser 2016, 18).

Conclusion

Emphasising the significance of cultural codes and discourses in shaping the lived experience of illness is central to a postmodern biocultural understanding of health and illness. The way in which illness conditions get represented in the mainstream cultural discourses determines not only the collective notions of illness but also the sufferers' conceptualisations of the ill self. Popular cultural media, such as films, novels, advertisements, and TV shows, circulate multiple perspectives on illness which cumulatively generate cultural ideologies of health and illness. Representations of conditions such as AIDS, cancer, and mental disorders in pop culture are often stereotypical, regressive, and misleading. Such negative portrayals reinforce cultural stigma which affects the victims adversely. In this context, investigating the popular cultural representations of female infertility reveals that popular texts mostly perpetuate and reaffirm dominant stereotypes, normative perceptions, and essentialist perspectives surrounding women's childlessness. While the valorisation of motherhood by women's magazines and their subsequent stigmatisation of infertility offer historical evidence of flawed popular representations of the problem, contemporary novels testify how pop culture represents infertile women as greedy, psychotic, and sexually unappealing. TV melodramas routinely depict childless women as neurotic and vulnerable, often blaming their prioritising of education and career as the reasons for their infertile predicament. Striking parallels could be identified in egg-freezing advertisements' rhetoric of choice and blame, which suggests that infertility is self-inflicted since modern women have adequate choice with the advancements in reproductive technology. Worse still, horror movies and infertility reality TV project the image of infertile women as figurations of monstrosity. Such marginalising and scientifically unfounded portrayals reinforce mainstream myths and stereotypes on infertility and inflict severe psychic and social harm to the childless women.

Notably, women's infertility memoirs create a counter-discourse to popular culture's stigmatising representations of childlessness. Foregrounding the experiential realities of their suffering, memoirists provide a realistic and honest depiction of their condition and its attendant challenges. Such uniquely personal accounts of infertility not only counteract popular myths and stereotypes but also document the personal, social, and medical aspects of navigating infertility with brutal honesty. Arguably, as a counter-narrative to popular culture, infertility memoirs destigmatise female infertility, and, in the process, reclaim agency and voice for the sufferers. In this context, the proliferation of women's graphic memoirs on infertility not only enriches the body of life narratives on childlessness but also extends subjective and nuanced explorations of infertility to the visual medium of comics.

Notes

1 The term "gender advertisements" denotes images in advertising portraying stereotypical and regressive gender roles and displays.
2 Egg freezing (or mature oocyte cryopreservation) is an egg-preserving procedure to enable women to get pregnant in the future. The process involves harvesting eggs from a woman's ovary, which "are frozen unfertilised and stored for later use" (Mayo Clinic 2019).
3 "Infertility reality TV shows" analysed here include American reality shows which have infertility and infertility treatment as one of the storylines in at least two episodes.
4 RESOLVE is a national fertility association established in the US in 1974 which aims to support and empower couples suffering from infertility.
5 Here, Couser combines the terms "quality of life" and "life writing" to create the portmanteau word "quality of life writing" (Couser 2016, 8).

References

Alden, Paulette Bates. 1996. *Crossing the Moon*. St. Paul, MN: Ruminator Books.
Allen, Debbie, dir. 2011. "Not Responsible." *Grey's Anatomy*. Burbank, CA: ABC Studios, Netflix.
Behuniak, Susan M. 2011. "The Living Dead? The Construction of People with Alzheimer's Disease as Zombies." *Ageing and Society* 31(1): 70–92. doi:10.1017/S0144686X10000693.
Benshoff, Harry M. 1997. *Monsters in the Closet: Homosexuality and the Horror Film*. Manchester: Manchester University Press.
Boer, Marjolein Lotte De, Cristina Archetti, and Kari Nyheim Solbraekke. 2019. "In/Fertile Monsters: The Emancipatory Significance of Representations of Women on Infertility Reality TV." *Journal of Medical Humanities*. doi:10.1007/s10912-019-09555-z.
Boggs, Belle. 2016. *The Art of Waiting: On Fertility, Medicine, and Motherhood*. Minneapolis, MN: Graywolf Press.
Clarke, Cath. 2018. "Private Life Review – Netflix Fertility Comedy is Painfully Funny." The *Guardian*, 5 October. www.theguardian.com/film/2018/oct/05/private-life-review-netflix-fertility-comedy-paul-giamatti. Accessed 15 September 2020.
Couser, Thomas. 2016. "Body Language: Illness, Disability, and Life Writing." *Life Writing* 13(1): 3–10. doi:10.1080/14484528.2016.1132376.
Edge, Brooke Weihe. 2015. "Barren or Bountiful? Analysis of Cultural Values in Popular Media Representations of Infertility." PhD diss., University of Colorado Boulder.
Fosket, Jennifer R., Angela Karran, and Christine LaFia. 2000. "Breast Cancer in Popular Women's Magazines from 1913 to 1996." In *Breast Cancer: Society Shapes an Epidemic*, ed. Anne S. Kasper and Susan J. Ferguson, 303–323. New York: St Martin's Press.

Ganev, Robin. 2017. "What we Mean When we Talk about Infertility." *The Walrus*, 6 April. https://thewalrus.ca/what-we-mean-when-we-talk-about-infertility/. Accessed 20 August 2020.

Gaviola, Karen, dir. 2011. "What we Have Here." *Private Practice*. Burbank, CA: ABC Studios, Netflix.

Gilman, Sander 1982. *Seeing the Insane*. New York: John Wiley.

Gilman, Sander. 1988. *Disease and Representation: Images of Illness from Madness to AIDS*. Ithaca, NY: Cornell University Press.

Gilman, Sander. 2014. "Seeing Bodies in Pain." In *Health Humanities Reader*, ed. Therese Jones, Delese Wear, and Lester D. Friedman, 171–175. New Brunswick, NJ: Rutgers University Press.

Grossman, Michael, dir. 2007. "The Other Side of This Life Part 2." *Grey's Anatomy*. Burbank, CA: ABC Studios, Netflix.

Hall, Stuart. 1995. "The Whites of their Eyes: Racist Ideologies and the Media." In *Gender, Race and Class in Media*, ed. G. Dines and J. Humez, 89–93. London: Sage.

Harvey, Dee. 2019. "Eggs Age over Time." *Media Res: A MediaCommons Project*, 3 September. http://mediacommons.org/imr/content/infertility-failure-egg-freezing-advertisements-and-myth-having-it-all. Accessed 15 May 2020.

James, P. D. 1994. *The Children of Men*. New York: Warner Books.

Jayadevan, Anitha. 2009. *Malicious Medicine: My Experience with Fraud and Falsehood in Infertility Clinics*. New Delhi: Penguin Books India.

Jenkins, Henry, Tara McPherson, and Jane Shattuc. 2002. "Defining Popular Culture." In *The Politics and Pleasures of Popular Culture*, ed. Henry Jenkins, Tara McPherson, and Jane Shattuc, 26–42. Durham, NC: Duke University Press.

Jenkins, Tamara, dir. 2018. *Private Life*, Netflix.

Johnson, Malynnda A. 2013. "More than Pop Culture: Depictions of HIV in the Media and the Effect on Viewer's Perception of Risk." *Journal of Homosexuality* 60(8): 1117–1142. doi:10.1080/00918369.2013.776423.

Katkin, Elizabeth. 2019. *Conceivability: What I Learned Exploring the Frontiers of Fertility*. New York: Simon & Schuster.

Loughran, Tracey. 2017. "Conditions of Illusion: Agency, Feminism, and Cultural Representations of Infertility in Britain, c. 1960–80." In *The Palgrave Handbook of Infertility in History: Approaches, Contexts and Perspectives*, ed. Gayle Davis and Tracey Loughran, 431–460. London: Palgrave Macmillan.

Lupton, Deborah. 2003. *Medicine as Culture: Illness, Disease and the Body in Western Societies*. London: Sage.

Lynch, Karen Danna. 2005. "Advertising Motherhood: Image, Ideology, and Consumption." *Berkeley Journal of Sociology* 49: 32–57. www.jstor.org/stable/41035601.

Marsh, Margaret, and Wanda Romer. 1996. *The Empty Cradle: Infertility in America from Colonial Times to the Present*. Baltimore, MD: Johns Hopkins University Press.

Mayo Clinic. 2019. "Egg Freezing." 1 February. www.mayoclinic.org/tests-procedures/egg-freezing/about/pac-20384556. Accessed 15 May 2020.

Micks, Callie. 2019. *The Baby Binder*. Maitland Colonnades, FL: Mill City Press.

Misiano, Christopher, dir. 2007. "Testing 1-2-3." *Grey's Anatomy*. Burbank, CA: ABC Studios, Netflix.

Morris, David B. 1998. *Illness and Culture in the Postmodern Age*. Berkeley: University of California Press.

Morris, David B. 2000. "How to Speak Postmodern: Medicine, Illness, and Cultural Change." *The Hastings Center Report* 30(6): 7–16. doi:10.2307/3528447.

Munthe, Emma Gray. 2020. "HIV and AIDS in the Movies." Face of AIDS Film Archive. 17 January. https://faceofaids.ki.se/theme/women-and-aids/hiv-and-aids-in-the-movies. Accessed 15 May 2020.

Proops, Marjorie. 1967. "Counselling-in-the-Round." *Woman*, 14 October.

Scully, Anne-Marie. 2014. *Motherhoodwinked: An Infertility Memoir*. South Carolina: CreateSpace Independent Publishing Platform.

Shigley, Sally Bishop. "Great Expectations: Infertility, Disability, and Possibility." In *The Palgrave Handbook of Infertility in History: Approaches, Contexts and Perspectives*, ed. Gayle Davis and Tracey Loughran, 37–55. London: Palgrave Macmillan.

Sims, David. 2018. "Netflix's Private Life is Brutal, Honest, and Brilliant." *The Atlantic,* 4 October. www.theatlantic.com/entertainment/archive/2018/10/private-life-review/571780/. Accessed 17 August 2020.

Sontag, Susan. 1978. *Illness as Metaphor*. New York: Farrar, Straus & Giroux.

Sontag, Susan. 1989. *AIDS and Its Metaphors*. New York: Anchor.

Tenreyro, Tatiana. 2018. "This Netflix Drama Explores an Aspect of Motherhood that's Rarely Seen Onscreen." *Bustle,* 5 October. www.bustle.com/p/is-private-life-a-true-story-the-netflix-movie-explores-aspect-of-motherhood-thats-rarely-seen-onscreen-12155368. Accessed 19 September 2020.

Williamson, Rachel. 2019. "Infertility as Failure: Egg Freezing Advertisements and the Myth of 'Having it All.'" *Media Res: A MediaCommons Project*, 3 September. http://mediacommons.org/imr/content/infertility-failure-egg-freezing-advertisements-and-myth-having-it-all. Accessed 15 May 2020.

Woman's Own. 1962. "Marlene Dietrich's ABC." 6 October, p. 16.

YouTube. 2016. "Extend Fertility: It's your Life and Plan." 5 October. www.youtube.com/watch?v=eRCg8bO1bOk. Accessed 15 May 2020.

3 Hegemonic creations
Pronatalism and the social construction of motherhood

Introduction

Defining female identity primarily in terms of their childbearing capacity is prevalent across cultures. Centrality of motherhood within discursive formations of womanhood has resulted in inextricable linkages between maternity and femininity. The reproductive ethic privileged by socio-cultural discourses and institutions, which are impelled by the pervasive ideology of pronatalism, coerces women to procreate, reducing their identity to mere reproducing bodies. Consequently, those who are unable to reproduce due to fertility-related disorders encounter severe cultural derision and social stigmatisation. In a close reading of Paula Knight's graphic memoir, *The Facts of Life*, this chapter aims to investigate how the pluripotent space of the comics medium allows the author to arraign the ideology of pronatalism as an oppressive force that mediates her lived experience of infertility. Drawing theoretical insights from Ellen Peck, Judith Senderowitz, and Ann Snitow, among others, the chapter also seeks to examine the socially constructed and gendered nature of motherhood as it unfolds in Knight's narrative.

Pronatalism and the social construction of motherhood

Ellen Peck and Judith Senderowitz in their "Introduction" to *Pronatalism: The Myth of Mom and Apple Pie* (1974) frame pronatalism[1] as a "strong and heretofore unquestioned social force which has produced both the universal-parenthood ideal and its attendant discriminations" (9) because "reproduction in all cultures has been accepted as central to identity, immorality and survival" (1). Notably, pronatalist thought, which permeates and undergirds state policies and the everyday practices of cultural discourses and institutions (such as

DOI: 10.4324/9781003028628-4

family, religion, and education), situates procreation as fundamental to their ideological framework. Such coercive and persuasive enforcement of the reproductive ethic not only deprives individuals of their freedom to make reproductive choices but also constructs a rigid social value system centred around procreation. As Laura Carroll observes in her *The Baby Matrix* (2012), pronatalism includes "a collection of beliefs so embedded that they have come to be seen as 'true'" (7), and a cardinal premise in pronatalist thought is the supposition that "woman's role must involve maternity – that woman's destiny and fulfilment are closely wedded to the *natal*, or birth, experience" (Peck and Senderowitz 1974, 1). Worse still, by situating womanhood within the constraints of reproduction, socio-cultural and political apparatuses of pronatalist ideology not only reduce women to their procreative role but also diminish them to a mere "uterus ... and a directing personality" (2). Enforcing motherhood as central to a woman's identity through images, representations, and constructions of the maternal, usually perpetuated and enforced through mainstream cultural scripts, is the extant *modus operandi* of the pronatalist project. Such unwarranted valorisation of childbirth and mothering as the most venerable of a woman's gender roles devalues "*woman as womb*" (2). Apparently, this entwining of the maternal and the feminine has led to the forced normalisation and institutionalisation of motherhood "as a natural outcome of biologically given gender differences ... and as a natural manifestation of an innate female characteristic, namely the maternal instinct" (Smart 1996, 37).

Contemporary socio-cultural formations are rife with the notion that "[t]he only truly enlightened choice to make as a woman, the one that proves, first, that you are a 'real' woman, and second, that you are decent, worthy one is to become a 'mom'" (Douglas and Michaels 2004, 5). To use Melanine Notkin's term, the present-day socio-cultural landscape is "mom-opic," with a myopic perception of womanhood as motherhood (Notkin 2016). This renewed idealisation of motherhood or "frenetic maternalism" in the twenty-first century may be attributed to "economic precarity, a resurgence of reactionary politics in the west, the fragility of the nuclear family, crises of masculinity, an ageing population and a backlash against feminism" (Rodgers 2018, 86). Given such varied and numerous reasons, pronatalism remains a predominant operative force with its ideological entwining of the maternal and the feminine in the contemporary era.

Hegemonic and normative construction of motherhood stigmatises those who choose not to have children as well as infertile women at large. To quote Julie Rodgers, "so strong is the conflation of motherhood with 'real' womanhood that the non-mother's identity is not simply marginal, but practically invisible" (Rodgers 2018, 88). Additionally, the wider public discourse of maternalism circulates negative and fallacious assumptions about non-motherhood because "culture has always feared the childless woman ... as a destabilizing and potentially radical figure" (Day 2012). Such cultural scripts generate the image of the childless as an abomination, and their lives are invariably projected as "emotionally stunted and unfulfilling" (Lewis 2015, 31).

Despite pronatalism remaining an ideological constraint for an independent female identity, women's liberation movements and feminism have not so far attempted a thorough critique of its restrictive designs. Illustrative of this glaring oversight, Ann Snitow cites her own predicament as a childless woman and faults feminist theory:

> I want to criticize the pervasive pronatalism that has so shaped my recent experience – a pronatalism not only in the culture at large but also inside feminism ... feminist culture didn't seem to be producing alluring images or thinkable identities for the childless.
>
> (Snitow 1992, 32)

In a similar vein, Peck and Senderowitz argue that, though

> feminism has developed as a movement with the goal of removing past restraints on women's roles, image, and identity ... it has not emphasised pronatalist constraints ... [and] a probable forthcoming feminist development will be an increased emphasis on freedom to choose not to bear children.
>
> (Peck and Senderowitz 1974, 8)

Given such a background, contemporary feminist enunciations require a textual space for the childless whose voices are marginalised within the constraining discourses of pronatalism and motherhood. Knight's autopathography on involuntary childlessness, in which she challenges the normative structures of the maternal and the feminine through an enunciation of the subjective realities of infertility, is a cultural work in that direction. Knitting together the author's subjective realities of being an infertile woman in a society that equates womanhood with motherhood and family with children, *The Facts of Life* lays bare the patriarchal and misogynistic nature of pronatalist institutions/discourses that enervate and stigmatise the childless.

"NO! THIS way!": girl child as a pronatalist subject

Knight begins her memoir with an elaborate account of the birth and early upbringing of her alter ego Polly. Deftly weaving the personal with the political, the author annotates her birth year 1969 as historically significant, with a flow chart that depicts developments such as Apollo 11 and a women's equal pay demonstration at Trafalgar Square. The epicentre of the chart reads thus: "[s]ince 1961, the contraceptive pill had become more available on the NHS – mainly for married women," enabling women to "delay childbearing" or to "forgo sprouting in favour of education and career" (2017, 14). Ironically, the socio-scientific and medical progress ushered in by modernity had little bearing on the everyday realities of women like Polly who are deeply implicated in the pronatalist myth of motherhood. Though women's liberation movements (such as represented by the Trafalgar Square demonstration) and medical advancements including the invention of the contraceptive pill sought to neutralise gender inequalities, women's identity and self-fulfilment were still wedded to their maternal role. Elsewhere, the author laments this deplorable contradiction: "[i]n the 1970s, it was still expected that the main goal of a girl would be to get married and have children when she grew up – at least that's what people frequently told you would happen" (18).

Exploiting the semiotic and multimodal potency of the comics medium, which involves a creative combination of visual and verbal enunciations, Knight offers a graphic exposition to this cultural conundrum (see Figure 3.1). In two adjacent yet interconnected short panels, the author depicts the naturalisation of gender roles when young girls are

Figure 3.1 Paula Knight, *The Facts of Life* (Myriad, 2017), 18.

56 Hegemonic creations

invariably coerced into future motherhood. While the first panel pictures Polly as a little girl carrying baby dolls, the second panel imagines her as a mother carrying children. The interconnectedness of the two panels signifies how in a culture that inextricably associates womanhood with motherhood, the transformation from a girl to an adult woman inevitably means carrying children instead of baby dolls. Interestingly, the little girl in the second panel is also depicted as carrying a baby doll, an omen of her inevitable future motherhood.

Elsewhere, the memoir portrays Polly's obsessive attachment to baby dolls when she imaginatively assumes being the mother of her dolls while playing with her childhood friend April (2017, 22). Knight's deployment of baby dolls has cultural resonances in that little girls are "encouraged to play with dolls – to play at motherhood" (Peck and Senderowitz 1974, 2). The doll turns into an interpellative tool of the pronatalist ideology. Simone de Beauvoir in *The Second Sex* delineates how dolls as playthings perform the ideological function of engendering in the girl child notions of femininity and motherhood. As de Beauvoir rightly argues, the little girl simultaneously identifies with the doll and assumes its parenthood: "[t]he doll is not only her double; it is also her child ... She confides in her doll, she brings it up ... Which is to say she experiences subjective affirmation and identification through the doll" (de Beauvoir 1953, 286–287).

The memoir also illustrates how institutional spaces and practices that adhere to the mainstream reproductive ethic produce gendered subjectivities. Here it is apposite to examine the way in which social institutions are made into apparatuses of coercion by the dominant ideological forces. Ideology, according to Louis Althusser, operates through what he terms "ideological state apparatuses," such as educational institutions, religious organisations, family, and the media, which interpellate individuals as subjects (Althusser 1971, 136–138). Drawing upon the Althusserian formulation of ideology, Judith Butler affirms that gender identities are constructed within such ostensibly apolitical social formations where the girl child is "girled" (Butler 1993, 7–8). Interestingly, Butler's notion of ideological interpellation in gender theory is partly inspired by de Beauvoir's formulation that "feminine" is not a natural condition but a form of "becoming" through cultural conditioning. To quote de Beauvoir, "[o]ne is not born, but rather becomes a woman ... It is civilization as a whole that produces this creature ... which is described as feminine" (de Beauvoir 1953, 273).

Read through such a theoretical lens, Knight's narrative delineates the ideological interpellations within social formations that manipulate individuals into subjects of pronatalism. In particular, the author foregrounds the role of family in this enterprise through a rendition of her traditional upbringing within a gendered domesticity. Knight pictures Polly as a little girl listening to her parents' conversation at the dinner table about one of their acquaintances "selling her house for fifteen thousand pounds!" (2017, 17). The conversation creates a profound impact in Polly's psyche as she worriedly asks her mother, "[h]ow will I ever have enough money to buy a whole house?" (17). The mother replies to the little girl, "[o]hh – don't go worrying about all that! You'll have a husband and he will have a job – so he'll help to buy it! He'll earn the money and you'll be at home looking after your children" (17). Little Polly is seen in the kitchen helping her mother in cleaning the utensils, and towards the end of their conversation her small visage is depicted as half shadowed by the stack of dinner plates. Thus the scene illustrates how the girl child is subjected to the pronatalist interpellation within the gendered space of the family while she is trained/made to believe that marriage and childrearing are her only destiny to realise her aspirations. It also demonstrates the way in which a gendered domesticity reinforces the binaries of the private/public mapped onto woman/man.

As such, Knight's narrative exposes how the pronatalist ideology percolates through other institutions and discourses including education, medicine, and the media, thereby shaping the mental landscape of the subject. Illustrating the prevalence of pronatalism in the classroom, Polly laments how in her biology class reproduction "was all about the sperm and the egg, and what happens when the woman gets pregnant" (2017, 43). According to the textbooks, "[t]he purpose of coitus was for fertilisation. No mention of recreation, or of contraception" (43). At a later stage, Polly recollects a scene from her biology class on reproductive health, where it was never "OK not to have children" (199). Evidently education works here as an ideological apparatus of pronatalism, making the children internalise its logic through persuasive conditioning. In a similar vein, the author bemoans the pronatalist prejudices within the discourse of medicine while narrating her childhood experience of listening to a doctor on television for whom "the most important thing in life is having children" (33). Elsewhere, accentuating the role of the media in shaping her attitudes towards (m)otherhood as a young girl, Knight recollects listening to the song "I've Never Been to Me" (1982), which was "a lament by a lonely woman who had regrets about not having had kids" (47). In a Commentary, Knight clarifies the impact of the song in her teenage psyche:

> [l]ooking back, the song contains some of the most pronatal lyrics I've ever heard ... Because I liked the song at such a delicate

formative age, it must surely have had some kind of subconscious influence over a fear of ending up childless and lonely.

(Coxon 2018)

Thus, the author succeeds in portraying the pervasiveness of pronatalism in the socio-cultural context of Polly's upbringing, coercing her to submit to its conditioning.

Knight here attempts a pictorial rendition of the protagonist's internalisation of pronatalist values perpetuated through various socio-scientific apparatuses (see Figure 3.2). The first panel succinctly portrays the ideologically mediated psychic landscape of little Polly as it carries a fairy-tale image of a married couple. Interestingly, the panel contains words written in capitals: "HUSBAND" and "HOUSE" (2017, 19). Suggesting that the scene is an imaginative rendition of the protagonist's mental make-up, which is conditioned by the dominant ideology, an angel is seen leading the couple to their heavenly abode. Likewise, the subsequent panel diagrams Polly's mental frame and is filled with words and phrases (such as "married," "husband," "house," and "when you have a little girl") related to marriage, motherhood, and domesticity (19).

The third panel, where the narration takes a detour from the previous scenes, depicts Polly as a young woman watching her imaginary daughter riding a toy horse. The scene is an imaginary recreation of Polly's own childhood experience of riding on a toy horse, when her mother proposes that "[w]hen you have bairns, they'll be able to play on this, too!" (Knight 2017, 16). In fact, such pronatalist utterances and citations ("when you grow up and have children of your own …") often engender in children "an early impression of the inevitability of parenthood" (Peck and Senderowitz 1974, 2). Reminded of her mother's pronatalist overtures, Polly observes, "[t]hese seemingly benign little words are only the same as many people have traditionally said to their children. Would I do it differently?" (Knight 2017, 19). Resisting such discursive interpellations, the protagonist corrects herself: "[w]hen … er … IF you have bairns, they'll be able to play on this, too!" (19). Projecting herself as a victim of ostensibly harmless pronatalist propositions, the author reminds readers of the role of language and its ideological effect in the creation of gendered subjectivities.

Returning to the theme of the girl child's socially conditioned pronatalist mental make-up, Knight draws two borderless panels to map Polly's neural pathways. The author illustrates how the protagonist's childhood psyche is laced with the notions of marriage and childrearing, which later constrain her to disavow a pronatalist life

Hegemonic creations 59

Figure 3.2 Paula Knight, *The Facts of Life* (Myriad, 2017), 19.

course in adulthood. In particular, the metaphorically loaded last panel depicts an adult Polly attempting to defy the social expectations of her gender, venturing a tightrope walk through an alternative path only to be interrupted by the angel, who coerces her to the pronatalist path ("NO!! THIS way!!"). Lamenting her predicament, the author observes, "[t]hese neural pathways would be so well-trodden by adulthood that any diversion would feel precarious" (2017, 19). Here, Knight's deployment of the angel as a metaphor of ideological interpellation resonates with Virginia Woolf's use of angel imagery in "Professions for Women" to signify the role of the dominant ideology in manipulating women to be the "angels in the household". In essence, the narrative illustrates the role of ideological apparatuses including family and education in a girl child's pronatalist subjectification. Citing the subjective experiences of her upbringing, the author arraigns the socio-cultural instruments of pronatalism that mediate and dominate her mental landscape in myriad ways.

"We're in the club!": childlessness and cultural otherhood

Dramatising the private/public tensions at work within the discourses of pronatalism and (m)otherhood, *The Facts of Life* limns how the protagonist's ideologically imposed pronatalist subjectivity stipulates that she follow the socially sanctioned pathway of marriage and motherhood. The author especially depicts herself succumbing to such ideologically mediated gender expectations as Polly marries and chooses to have a baby. Yet after repeated miscarriages and the failure of medical interventions including IVF to produce any desired results, Polly and her partner Jack decide to "cease pursuing parenthood" (Knight 2017, 196). Here, the narrative deftly delineates the complex process of social stigmatisation and cultural othering through which Polly's childlessness/non-motherhood is perceived, questioned, and bemoaned by the dominant pronatalist socio-cultural matrix, which essentially aggravates her predicament. Alluding to the cultural backlash on her non-parenthood, Polly laments: "[t]ogether we were gaining confidence in our decision. But the outside world would prove more of a challenge" (196).

As such, the narrative demonstrates the cultural valorisation of childrearing, which would inevitably ostracise the childless, through a visual juxtaposition of the contrasting social reactions to the news of the protagonist's parenthood/non-parenthood. The author imagines reactions from Polly's family and friends at the news of her pregnancy: the protagonist is pictured at the centre of the panel, emotionally fulfilled and content, holding her pregnant belly as she receives words of appreciation ("Congratulations," "Hurrah!," "Fantastic news!," "Wow!," "I'm so happy for you both!") along with gifts and a bouquet. Interestingly, Knight fills the background of the panel with the ideograph of the heart, conveying the love and warmth that the news of pregnancy engenders in others. Returning to reality and referring to her inability to reproduce, Knight laments: "I'd never experience the joy of imparting what society celebrates as the ultimate good news" (2017, 197). Here the narrative problematises the cultural obsession with parenthood "as the ultimate good news," which invariably frames the infertile as social misfits.

The succeeding panels illustrate the protagonist's real experience of conveying to others the decision to give up the pursuit of parenthood. When Polly confides to a friend that she has "decided to stop trying," the friend responds: "I'm worried you might REGRET it!!" (Knight 2017, 197). Ironically, Polly's friend is pictured being annoyed by her children as one of them pulls her hair from behind, making her almost fall. Having witnessed her friend's travails of motherhood, Polly comments in a sarcastic vein: "[a]nd surely it's better to regret *not* having children than it is to regret having them" (197). At the level of form, the scene is particularly striking in that the author successfully maps into the panel borders the mounting tension between her personal self and the social world. Though both Polly and her friend converse sitting opposite to each other at a coffee table, they are depicted in two separate panels with the gutter dividing the table (197). The gutter thus denotes the unbridgeable chasm between Polly and her friend, who is representative of the larger pronatalist society.

Knight continues to foreground the stigmatising nature of Polly's culturally mediated infertility experiences, in which "[t]he world's preoccupation with breeding status had to be negotiated at every turn" (2017, 201). Replete with several such instances, the narrative illustrates how the protagonist was made to feel inadequate by friends, family, and acquaintances who mindlessly offered child-centric solutions. For instance, when the subject of a casual conversation with an acquaintance gradually turns to childrearing, Polly's estrangement is signified in the form of a crack that appears in the panel. Tellingly, Polly predicts the course of the conversation: "[s]he's going to tell me I can adopt next" (202). As the discourse continues, the crack in the panel deepens, signifying the widening fissure between the two perspectives. Again, Polly's sense of isolation and stigma is pictorially conveyed as the panel eventually breaks in two, separating the protagonist from her friend. The fragmented panel pictures Polly amidst an unempathetic crowd that refuses to broaden its perspectives on childlessness. Elsewhere, reflecting on this social preoccupation with parenthood that leaves the infertile isolated, Knight laments: "[i]t seems that, once some people become parents, it can be hard to comprehend an alternate path to fulfilment" (198).

In such a context, the role of the mainstream media and popular culture in constituting a collective imaginary of women finding self-fulfilment through motherhood cannot be understated. To quote Katherine Kinnick, the mainstream media and popular culture "idealize and glamorize motherhood as the one path to fulfilment for women" (Kinnick 2009, 3). Such eulogised, imaginative constructions of parenthood proffered in the media "have a profound impact on women who do not have children" (Heffernan and Wilgus 2018, 1). It is not surprising that Knight's memoir is critical of the exaltation of parenthood, specifically motherhood, in the mainstream media and popular culture, as they not only shape and reinforce cultural attitudes towards childlessness but also aggravate the plight of non-mothers. Alluding to such stereotypical representations, the author observes: "[a]s a person without kids, you must prepare to be effaced in a society where 'family' means 'children'" (Knight 2017, 205).

Knight is particularly sceptical of the "normative and marginalising nature of advertising" (2017, 206), as it simultaneously reflects and shapes cultural attitudes towards parenthood. In an interview, the author clarifies how advertisements stigmatise marginal subjectivities: "[u]nfortunately, we live in an excessive consumer society … we are slaves to advertising and presentations of what a good life resembles. This can result in feelings of marginalisation and inadequacy if yours doesn't resemble it" (Ayres 2017). Illustrating, as it were, the pernicious impact of advertisements, Polly is seen staring at a giant billboard, which essentialises happy "hardworking families" as consisting of parents, children, and a pet (see Figure 3.3). Elsewhere, as an attempt to challenge such heteronormative and pronatalist representations, the author caricatures alternative family models devoid of children, including a homosexual couple (Knight 2017, 206–207).

The narrative also foregrounds the pronatal sentiments that undergird the media's preoccupation with celebrity pregnancies in that the memoirist includes popular magazine covers with sensational reports on "BABY BULGE" and "IVF success" stories of rich celebrities. According to the author, "[c]elebrity magazines obsess over baby bumps and boyfriends – rather than how hardworking, financially independent and successful those women are" (Melia 2017). In fact, the private lives of female celebrities are relentlessly scrutinised by tabloids, which ascribe little importance to their success as career women. Knight empathises with a popular actor's predicament: "[t]his actress is the same age as me. Over the years, I'd grown tired of the media preoccupation with her childlessness and assumptions over her every fretful expression. Couldn't they let her just be an actress?" (Knight 2017, 205).

Hegemonic creations 63

Figure 3.3 Paula Knight, *The Facts of Life* (Myriad, 2017), 205.

Adopting a symbolic vocabulary, Knight visually sums up how infertile women are subjected to social othering through media representations that have thrust motherhood into public consciousness (see Figure 3.3). Accordingly, the first panel pictures three pregnant women who represent three dominant races (black, brown, and white), happily announcing in a single voice, "we are in the club" (Knight 2017, 205), with the letter "M" written in bold denoting their singular identity as happy mothers. The next panel portrays Polly turning her head away from the previous panel and stating, "didn't want to join anyway" (205). Signifying the ostracising nature of those representations, the second panel has the word "other" written in bold as a continuation of the letter "M" of the previous panel, which read together constitute "(M) other." Here the image of pregnant women forming a club of their own as self-fulfilled individuals not only alienates non-mothers like Polly but also inscribes "otherhood" on them. Notably, the idea of the childless as the cultural other is recurrent in Knight's narrative. In one of the early establishing shots, Knight pictures herself inside her car looking at a hospital vehicle with "mother care" painted on its body (6). As a visual play, the succeeding middle shot captures only a part of the vehicle, showing "other care" instead of "mother care." This shift signifies the cultural politics of othering the childless that underwrite pronatalist discourses.

Striking as Knight's autopathography is, other graphic memoirs on female infertility echo Knight's critique of the valorisation of motherhood in popular culture and the mainstream media, which casts the childless in a negative light. In particular, Emily Steinberg in her *Broken Eggs* bemoans the cultural preoccupation with "mommy images": "we're saturated with paintings of the mother and child in art history … [p]resently, our culture is obsessed with babies and fecundity … Mommy blogs reign on the Net and the tabloids scream joyously at the merest hint of a 'baby bump' growing in the stomachs of forty-something celebs" (2014, n.p). Thus, Knight's arraignment of the mainstream media and pop culture in *The Facts of Life* for their essentialist imaginings of (m)otherhood galvanises and forms part of a larger critique that infertility life narratives undertake in the graphic medium.

"Let me out!": thinking beyond motherhood

Having undergone the social ridicule and othering occasioned by infertility, Polly ventures to investigate the ideological determinants that shape a society's propensity to equate womanhood and motherhood. Accordingly, Knight pictures Polly lying inside a bathtub (which also doubles as a panel), immersed in reading. The author elaborates her endeavour:

> I wanted to understand the historical background that led to present attitudes towards whether or not people have children. The

books I read helped me to gain a new perspective on, and comes to terms with, my own position in society.

(2017, 220)

Knight continues to trace the ideological history of pronatalism, which in the author's own terms is "a religious, political and cultural ideology that encourages people to reproduce" (220). The subsequent panels illustrate how religious texts and scriptures uphold the pronatalist ideology by exploiting believers' fear of damnation. The panels show a couple in the early phases of human civilisation (indicated by their premodern sartorial conventions) receiving a divine warning, ("[b]e fruitful and multiply (or else)!"), and blindly obeying it ("Yes, sir") (220). Further, Knight examines the reasons behind the societal tendency to eulogise pregnancy and motherhood: "[i]n a bid to encourage women to feel that motherhood was their destiny, the status of motherhood was elevated. Pregnancy and motherhood became sentimentalised" (220). In so doing, as Knight argues, the pronatalist culture invariably overshadowed the negative facets of pregnancy and childbearing. In a sarcastic heft, the author challenges the credibility of discourses that eulogise motherhood: "You never hear much about Mary dealing with Baby Jesus's stinky nappies, do you?" (220).

The next couple of panels juxtapose two strikingly contradictory images of conception and childbearing. While the first panel depicts a content mother carrying her baby, with haloes over their heads evoking the iconography of the Madonna and Child, the adjacent panel shows a young woman struggling with abdominal pain presumably caused by pregnancy-related issues. Notably, the woman in the second panel is surrounded by voices representing the dominant ideology of pronatalism, commanding her to "keep it [pain] quiet … or they won't breed" (Knight 2017, 221). Elsewhere, Knight explains why pronatalism silences discourses that foreground the negative aspects of pregnancy and childbirth: "I think it's also part of pronatal ideology – don't talk about pregnancy problems or they won't want to sprout" (Ayres 2017). Thus, the author critiques what she describes as "a conspiracy of silence over the dangers and problems regarding pregnancy, childbirth and the troubles associated with childbearing" (Knight 2017, 221).

Knight's account of the development of pronatalism also sheds light on how this pervasive ideology gets "manifested in policies that have corralled women's lives, but suited governments" (2017, 221). According to the author, women's life/work and reproductive choices are conveniently governed, mediated, and manipulated from time to time by various power structures, including patriarchy, the state, and capitalism, to suit their interests. To substantiate this, Knight observes how childcare was funded by the state during World War II (when women's labour was required) but the provision was conveniently removed after the war.

The narrative does not limit itself to delineating the negative effects of pronatalism in the realm of the personal alone, as it also depicts the plight of the Earth reeling under overpopulation. The author wonders how the ideology of pronatalism still thrives despite "world's population heading towards 9bn by 2040" (Knight 2017, 222). Dwelling on the possible reasons for this paradox, Knight arraigns religion (which preaches that "childless couples are selfish!"), governments, and capitalism, which require "future flock," "future voters and taxpayers," and "future consumers of stuff and resources" (222), respectively. Evidently women's reproductive choices, rather than being a personal affair, are largely mediated and manipulated by these forces, which are driven by selfish and pecuniary interests. Here the memoir exposes the agendas of various power structures, including religion and capitalism, in upholding and propagating the ideology of pronatalism.

As Knight's critique rightly evidences, a ubiquitous fixation with futurity undergirds the espousal of the pronatalist ideology by the state, religion, and capitalism. Speaking in the context of queer theory, Lee Edelman claims that futurity is almost always imagined in reproductive terms: culture and politics cannot "conceive of a future without the figure of the Child" (Edelman 2004, 11), and hence "Child" embodies "the telos of the social order" (11). Edelman deploys the term "reproductive futurism" to refer to an absolute privileging of heteronormativity based on futurity, which imposes an ideological limit on socio-political discourses in their envisioning of homosexuality and queerhood. What Edelman draws here is the coercive nature of such discursive frames, which essentially ostracise/nullify alternative possibilities that refuse to adhere to its logic. Parallels can be established between pronatalism and reproductive futurism in that they imagine social relations based on the logic of reproduction. Naturally, those who do not conform to the pronatal reproductive ethic are perceived as a threat to the normative social order and hence subject to ridicule and ostracisation. In this vein, the logic of futurity colludes with pronatalism in deeming infertile subjectivities marginal.

Echoing similar concerns, Knight pictures how "women's value to society is often judged on their relationship to children" (2017, 226). Accordingly, in the form of three sequential panels that look like tags, the narrative pictorially illustrates the social labelling through which women's identity is restricted to their maternal status. The first panel has the label "CAREER WOMAN," which is attached to those who prioritise their career over motherhood and hence don't have children. Knight laments that women are given such a label for carrying out their "human right to earn money" (226). While the second panel/label "CHILDLESS" signifies those who are unable to reproduce and hence are considered "incomplete," "not whole," and "something missing" (226), the succeeding panel includes the "CHILDFREE" women who are framed as "selfish" and "crazy" for choosing not to have children.

Illustrating the impact of such a social tagging (which collapses female identity and the maternal) on the protagonist's identity, the next couple of panels picture Polly in a quandary. Caught between "CHILDLESS?" and "CHILDFREE?," Polly reflects on her personal crisis: "I didn't feel I fitted any of the stereotypes. And I certainly didn't want to be defined as 'child'-anything" (Knight 2017, 227) (see Figure 3.4). The subsequent panels signify a defining moment in the memoir when the protagonist affirms her individuality and independent female identity through rejecting the social labelling of women using a pronatal vocabulary. Polly refuses to be labelled either childless or childfree as she responds to the question by concluding, "NEITHER, just ME" (227). Interestingly, Polly's response "untags" herself from the binary labelling of women as childfree and childless, as it literally defies the panel boundary by spreading across the panels (227).

The panels also show the protagonist as elated and emotionally fulfilled, pursuing her passion for art through drawing and music, unlike the previous panels, where she was seen as constricted (Knight 2017, 227). In an interview, the author clarifies her purpose behind the creation of the panels:

> I made 'Childless? Childfree? Neither, just me!' as a response to society's labelling of women without children rather than accepting them as autonomous human beings. I found a renewed sense of purpose and enthusiasm in my creative life, which was inextricable from my sense of self.
> (Ayres 2017)

Thus, the memoirist defies the social labels of non-motherhood imposed on her infertile subjectivity by the pronatal ideology by an affirmation of her independent personhood, thereby overcoming her predicament.

68 *Hegemonic creations*

Figure 3.4 Paula Knight, *The Facts of Life* (Myriad, 2017), 227.

Conclusion

As a health predicament with socio-cultural ramifications that can cause severe harm to women's identity and personhood, infertility summons subjective enunciations by sufferers. In such a context, Knight's *The Facts of Life* not only makes visible the author's victimisation and vulnerabilities as an infertile woman in a pronatal society but also interrogates the ideological forces that aggravate her crisis. Besides critiquing pronatalism and its attendant idealisation of the institution of motherhood, which constrains female identity, Knight illustrates the creation of pronatal subjectivities through ideological apparatuses including family and education. Specifically, the memoir launches a trenchant critique of the mainstream media and popular culture, which reinforce pronatal notions in the collective psyche, as it also delineates the complex mechanisms of social othering through which childless women are deemed marginal. Further, through an examination of the socio-cultural determinants of pronatalism, the author exposes the agendas of various power structures including the state, capitalism, and religion in their espousal of the pronatal ideology. A voice of defiance and self-affirmation emerges towards the end of the narrative when the protagonist rejects the social labelling of women based on their maternal status. Refusing to accept her victim status, the author celebrates her identity as an independent woman pursuing her passions.

Acknowledgements

This chapter is derived in part from an article published in the *Journal of Graphic Novels and Comics* on 20 May 2019 copyright Taylor & Francis, available online: www.tandfonline.com/10.1080/21504857.2019.1617179

Note

1 Ellen Peck and Judith Senderowitz define pronatalism as "any attitude or policy that is 'pro-birth', that encourages reproduction, that exalts the role of parenthood" (1974, 1).

References

Althusser, Louis. 1971. *Lenin and Philosophy, and Other Essays*, tr. B. Brewster. New York: Monthly Review Press.
Ayres, Andrea. 2017. "Marnie Galloway, Paula Knight and the Myth of Having it All – Part I." *Beat*, 14 December. www.comicsbeat.com/interview-marnie-galloway-paula-knight-the-myth-of-having-it-all-part-i. Accessed 18 October 2018.
Beauvoir, Simone de. 1953. *The Second Sex,* tr. H. M. Parshley. London: Jonathan Cape.
Butler, Judith. 1993. *Bodies that Matter: On the Discursive Limits of "Sex."* New York: Routledge.
Carroll, Laura. 2012. *The Baby Matrix: Why Freeing our Minds from Outmoded Thinking about Parenthood and Reproduction Will Create a Better World.* London: LiveTrue Books.

Coxon, Caitlin. 2018. "Paula Knight on the Facts of Life, Part II." Cardiff Book Talk, 12 February. https://cardiffbooktalk.org/2018/02/11/paula-knight-on-the-facts-of-life-part-ii. Accessed 16 October 2018.

Day, Jody. 2012. "Julia Gillard and the Fear of the Childless Woman." *The Guardian*, 25 October. www.theguardian.com/commentisfree/2012/oct/25/julia-gillard-childless-woman. Accessed 20 October 2016.

Douglas, Susan, and Meredith Michaels. 2004. *The Mommy Myth: The Idealization of Motherhood and How it has Undermined Women*. New York: Free Press.

Edelman, Lee. 2004. *No Future: Queer Theory and the Death Drive*. Durham, NC: Duke University Press.

Heffernan, Valerie, and Gay Wilgus. 2018. "Introduction: Imagining Motherhood in the Twenty-First Century – Images, Representations, Constructions." *Women: A Cultural Review* 29(1): 1–18. doi: 10.1080/09574042.2018.1442603.

Kinnick, Katherine. 2009. "Media Morality Tales and the Politics of Motherhood." In *Mommy Angst: Motherhood in American Popular Culture*, ed. Ann C. Hall and Mardia J. Bishop, 1–28. Santa Barbara, CA: Praeger/ABC-CLIO.

Knight, Paula. 2017. *The Facts of Life*. Oxford: Myriad.

Lewis, Helen. 2015. "The Motherhood Trap: Why are So Many Senior Female Politicians Childless?" *New Statesman*, 16 July. www.newstatesman.com/politics/2015/07/motherhood-trap. Accessed 16 August 2018.

Melia, Joe. 2017. "Interview: Paula Knight." *B24/7*, 9 March. www.bristol247.com/culture/books/interview-paula-knight-bristol/. Accessed 17 August 2018.

Notkin, Melanie. 2016. "The Most Undervalued Women in America are Childless Aunts." *New York Post*, 24 July. https://nypost.com/2016/07/24/the-most-undervalued-women-in-america-are-childless-aunts. Accessed 20 September 2018.

Peck, Ellen, and Judith Senderowitz. 1974. *Pronatalism: The Myth of Mom and Apple Pie*. New York: Crowell.

Rodgers, Julie. 2018. "On the Margins of Motherhood: Choosing to Be Child-Free in Lucie Joubert's *L'Envers Du Landau* (2010)." *Women: A Cultural Review* 29(1): 75–96. doi: 10.1080/09574042.2018.1425537.

Smart, Carol. 1996. "Deconstructing Motherhood." In *Good Enough Mothering? Feminist Perspectives on Lone Motherhood*, ed. Elizabeth Bortolaia Silva, 45–65. London: Routledge.

Snitow, Ann. 1992. "Feminism and Motherhood: An American Reading." *Feminist Review*. 40: 32–51. doi: 10.2307/1395276.

Steinberg, Emily. 2014. "Broken Eggs." *Cleaver*, 10 September. www.cleavermagazine.com/broken-eggs-by-emily-steinberg/. Accessed 20 April 2016.

4 The infertile body in the clinic
Medicalisation and loss of agency

Introduction

The ubiquitous power that the discourses and practices of medicine accrue as a result of the medicalisation of female reproduction deprives women of their autonomy over their reproductive body. In particular, invasive medical procedures deployed in the treatment of women's reproductive health quandaries such as infertility engender severe psychic-somatic turmoil in women, who are treated as damaged machines. The present chapter attempts to delineate the perils of medicalisation in the context of female infertility. The focus of the chapter is on the lack of female agency in the clinical experience of infertility, when the sufferer is reduced to the status of a docile body under the authoritative and penetrative medical eye. In a close reading of select graphic memoirs on women's infertility, including Phoebe Potts's *Good Eggs*, Emily Steinberg's *Broken Eggs*, Paula Knight's *The Facts of Life*, and Jenell Johnson's *Present/Perfect*, the chapter examines how the memoirists, using comics, subjectively foreground the hurt and estrangement they experience in a misogynist, and technologised system of infertility care. In so doing, the chapter argues, these graphic medicine narratives foreground nuanced issues such as loss of privacy, technological intrusion, and objectification that cause irreparable harm to women and jeopardise their identity as patients.

Feminist critique of medicalisation

Medical sociologists and cultural thinkers have developed a critique of medical hegemony through an examination of power relations in terms of medical knowledge and practice. Such a critique posits that "individuals' lives are profoundly experienced and understood through the discourses and practices of medicine and its allied professions" (Lupton

1997). In this context, the term medicalisation refers to the estranging, authoritative, and hegemonic nature of the medical discourses and practices. Critics contend that medicalisation allows the medical discourse to amass power and influence over its subjects, denying them autonomy and agency. A vital aspect of the medicalisation critique is the notion that "patients in general, because of their lack of medical knowledge, are placed in the position of vulnerable supplicants" (Lupton 1997, 96). Put differently, patients are "largely helpless, passive and disempowered, their agency crushed beneath the might of the medical profession" (97).

Taking cues from this line of argument, feminist approaches to medicine have developed a critique of patriarchal and misogynistic impulses that undergird medical attitudes towards women's health, specifically reproduction. According to feminist scholars of medicine, "Medical science has been one of the most powerful sources of sexist ideology in our culture" (Ehrenreich and English 1974), and they characterise the medical profession as a patriarchal institution that subjectifies women "by taking control over areas of women's lives such as pregnancy and childbirth that were previously the domain of female lay practitioners and midwives" (Lupton 1997, 97). As Deborah Steinberg (1990) states, "The history of medical science, particularly obstetrics and gynaecology, has been, on the one hand, the history of abuse and injury for women" (76). Again, Robbie Davis-Floyd (1992), in her analysis of American birth practices, argues that obstetrics operates with a "technocratic model of birth" that is predicated on "the weakness and inferiority of the female body, the validity of patriarchy, the superiority of science and technology, and the importance of institutions and machines" (152).

Accentuating the pervasive misogyny that undergirds the medical conceptualisations of pregnant bodies in purely mechanistic terms, Emily Martin contends that "women's bodies are often described in medical texts as if they were mechanical factories or centralized production systems" (2001, xi). According to Martin, medical procedures surrounding childbirth are predicated on the assumption that the womb and uterus form a mechanical pump that can expel the foetus. Further, in the evolution of surgical practices in obstetrics, "the metaphor of the uterus as a machine combines with the use of actual mechanical devices (such as forceps), which played a part in the replacement of female midwives' hands by male hands using tools" (Martin 2001, 54). Jennifer Shaw, in a similar vein, employs Michel Foucault's theorisation of the medical gaze as a guiding template to demonstrate how "the effort to make the interiors of the pregnant body visible in medical discourse was a crucial part of the development of the modern medical gaze" (2012, 110). According to Shaw, as pregnancy became increasingly medicalised, modern medicine began to treat the pregnant body as a sick body, leading to an "overlap of the pregnant and the pathological" (111). Delineating how this overlapping has led to a mechanistic treatment of the pregnant body discounting the lived aspect of pregnancy, Shaw observes: "The language of medical science has sought to be voice of the body without interference from the patient; this was true in both studies of pathology and in the gradual medicalisation of pregnancy" (111).

Like obstetrics and gynaecology, reproductive medicine has also been criticised by feminist scholars of medicine for blatant misogyny that undermines women's autonomy and agency. Specifically, examining reproductive medicine's treatment of female infertility, they observe that the "medical understandings of, and reactions to, infertility ha[ve] been shaped historically" and are "mediated by a range of social, political, and scientific factors" that are detrimental to women (Davis and Loughran 2017, 265). Cristina Pinheiro, in her analysis of ancient medical texts on the matter, notes that most of the medical accounts of female infertility are erroneous and entrenched in misogyny. For instance, Portuguese physician Rodrigo de Castro's influential text on women's medicine *De universa mulierum medicina* contains a section that relates female infertility "to masculine features such as a hoarse voice and thick black hair around the female genitalia, which were considered external signs of 'deviance'" (Davis and Loughran 2017, 266). Similarly, reflective of the medical anxieties surrounding female sexuality, many physicians in the past conceptualised "deviancy" by associating infertile women with hypersexuality and prostitution. Medical figures such as Claude-Martin Gardien developed a physiognomic portrait of infertile women to "advise husbands how to choose their ideal mate in order to guarantee a future fertile marriage" (266). Evidently, the medical discourse has internalised the patriarchal and misogynistic sentiments that underwrite most socio-cultural and scientific discourses in constructing the image of the infertile woman as a deviant category. In so doing, the discourses and practices of medicine have not only demonised the childless but also fractured their sense of the self and female identity.

Illustrating the impact of medicalisation on women in the context of reproductive medicine/infertility, Arthur L. Greil, in his "Infertile Bodies: Medicalisation, Metaphor, and Agency", notes that, for women, "medicalisation of infertility is a fait accompli" (2002, 101), and their bodies are "often subjected to the medical gaze" (101) "as *flawed* machines requiring expert intervention" (102). This is particularly significant since "authoritative knowledge concerning infertility has been deemed the province of medical specialists, who have the exclusive right and obligation to treat it in accordance with the institutional constraints of professional medicine" (102). Suffering from an illness condition like infertility, which threatens the integrity and sense of the self, women seek an immediate medical remedy. Additionally, the cultural mandate to reproduce and accept motherhood as an inevitable path towards fulfilment coerces infertile women to perceive medical intervention as a natural choice. However, "entering the medical system places these women in a paradoxical situation" (109), since "the experience of infertility treatment is an experience of frustration, loss of control, and mortification" (113). Foregrounding the deeply depersonalising nature of the clinical experience of infertility, Greil contends that most women experience infertility treatment "as an invasion of the integrity of the self" (109) and are "very critical of their physicians for ignoring the human side of healing" (110). Additionally, illustrative of the perils of the technologisation of medicine, particularly reproductive medicine, women are "pressured into making use of the new reproductive technologies" and hence can be "described as being exploited by these technologies [rather] than as taking advantage of them" (113). In essence, under the medical gaze, infertile women find themselves in "a situation in which, to recover their integrity, they [are] forced to participate in a system they perceive as a threat to that integrity" (110).

Contemporary feminist critique of reproductive medicine is centred primarily on the deployment of assisted reproductive technology (ART)[1] in the treatment of women's fertility-related quandaries. Feminist scholars interpret ART as "the latest chapter in the long history of the misappropriation of women's reproduction into androcentric Western understandings through techno-science, and medicine" (Lam 2015, 3). Accordingly, conceptive technologies "threaten women's reproductive autonomy" (47). Critics also refute the argument that deployment of ART in the treatment of female infertility could be empowering for women as it provides them with a reproductive choice by contending that ART extends "patriarchal control over female reproduction, exploiting it for power and profit" (48). Accentuating the role of medicine in social control, a theme extensively discussed by Foucault, they observe that ART, in the guise of rendering voice to women, "serve to mask industrial/social problems with therapy", and "it is because we now believe that ART can cure infertility that we believe it must be cured" (49). Extending this argument further, feminist scholar Patricia Spallone (1989) observes that contemporary practices in reproductive medicine underscore how "technology redefines the meaning of reproduction in society to the detriment of women, how technology sets a repressive ethic of reproduction, and in turn how repressive social relations provide the conditions for technology to happen" (4). In other words, increasing technologisation of infertility care through the deployment of ART alienates female patients, as it not only accords more power to medical professionals but also discounts patients' autonomy and agency.

Illustrating the ways in which the use of ART, specifically in vitro fertilisation (IVF), affects women adversely, Deborah Steinberg, in her "The Depersonalisation of Women through the Administration of 'In Vitro Fertilisation'" (1990), notes that IVF treatment involves an "unprecedented level of intervention, manipulation and reconstitution of women's bodies" (98). According to Steinberg, IVF procedures cause what she theorises as *erasure* and *recombination* in the female subject. While *erasure* refers to the processes that "obscure or remove women from recognition within the 'IVF' context", recombination includes the "effects of 'IVF' procedures on women: the alteration, removal and reconstitution of parts of or affecting women's whole bodies" (77). Hence, "within the context of IVF, *erasure* and *recombination* operate to depersonalise, that is to fragment, alienate and injure, women" (77). Steinberg also foregrounds how IVF procedures reinforce medical hegemony over women's bodies in that they are "not only *not* identified as agents of their reproduction, but they are not identified in any capacity; neither as participants nor, more specifically, as patients" (78). Further, referring to the intrusion and objectification that women experience during IVF, Steinberg observes that the procedure involves "an erosion of women's bodily and metaphysical privacy" (86), since it is "designed to maximise the bodily and personal visibility of women" (87). Arguably, this reflects medicine's refusal in "acknowledging or respecting *boundaries* to women's bodies and selves" (87). Put differently, the "imposed visibility" of women's bodies in IVF procedures causes a "literal and conceptual transfer of women's private domain (their bodies) into public commodities, the disembodied property of medical science" (86).

In essence, the discourses and practices of medicine, especially obstetrics, gynaecology, and reproductive medicine, which are concerned with women's reproductive lives, are arraigned by feminists for their inherent misogyny that reduces women to mere reproductive machines susceptible to medical gaze and control. In particular, the history of reproductive medicine reveals an insistent patriarchal bias that demonises infertile female subjectivity. Contemporary practices in infertility care are no way different in treating the childless as damaged objects that could be "opened, scrutinised, manipulated, parts extracted and then reintroduced" (86). Infertility treatment procedures thus constitute a constraining structure of care for women, for they not only constrict their reproductive agency but also abridge what Mary Daly (1979) describes as women's "Be-ing" – that is, women's ontological existence *free* from patriarchal control (2–7).

"The infertility death trap": *Broken Eggs* and *Present/Perfect*

Among women's graphic medical narratives on infertility, Emily Steinberg's memoir *Broken Eggs* centres primarily on the medical experience of infertility and brings into relief the plight of women who are being subjected to unsympathetic treatment by the medical establishment. The text lays bare the physical, psychological, and financial crises women must undergo inside an apathetic and exploitative system of infertility care. The author illustrates her predicament while undergoing treatment in the fertility clinic in a series of splash pages. On the first splash page, which depicts the memoirist's clinical experience of infertility, Steinberg portrays herself as a rodent emerging out of a cage (see Figure 4.1). The rodent is pictured as a half-human, half-animal figure, with a human head and an animal body. Notably, the rodent's human head bears an exact resemblance to the protagonist's, making her identification with the creature complete. Steinberg sums up her experience inside the clinic thus: "AND THEN I BECAME A **FERTILITY GUINEA PIG** GUINEA PIG". Here, the author uses the symbolic vocabulary of the caged rodent or the mouse trap to illustrate the dehumanising nature of her experience inside the infertility clinic – a cage in which she was trapped like a mouse. Steinberg also likens her predicament to that of a guniea pig in a science lab, where the animal is experimented upon by the scientists. The image, in essence, signifies how infertile women are treated as "human guinea pigs" (to borrow Bernard Shaw's phrase) trapped inside a cage-like fertility care, deprived of any agency.

Evidently, Steinberg deploys anthropomorphism, which was popularised by legendary artists like Art Spiegelman. The author's choice of the rodent metaphor to illustrate her victimhood in the hands of the medical establishment bears striking parallels with Spiegelman's picturing of the Jews as rats tortured by the cat-figured Nazis in *Maus* (1980). This suggests that the patient's experience in the clinic is similar to that of the Jews in the concentration camps, where they are reduced to the status of rats in the hands of their predators. Read in this way, it is not surprising that the author deems her encounter with infertility

The infertile body in the clinic 77

Figure 4.1 Emily Steinberg, *Broken Eggs* (Cleaver, 2014). n.p.

care as "THE FERTILITY DEATH TRAP". The metaphor of the rodent succeeds in illustrating the exploitative practices and the lack of agency that women experience inside hegemonic infertility care. The prey–predator dynamic that the author skilfully draws in as the subtext through the rodent metaphor signifies the power relations at work in the clinic, where the system and the professionals exercise absolute authority and control, relegating the patients' subjectivity to victimhood. Commenting on her estranging clinical encounter, Steinberg, in a personal email interview, states: "It was dehumanising, as I think a lot of medical procedures can be. You feel like a test subject. It turns a very intimate, personal, and loving act of creation into a mechanical, time sensitive series of stressed out experiments" (17 July 2019).

Steinberg's deployment of her "rodent-persona" as a visual metaphor of her predicament in the clinic also illustrates how authors of autobiographical comics deploy symbolic elements and rhetorical tropes while pictorially representing their physical identities to reflect their innermost sense of self, thereby adding layers of meaning to their self-portraits. Comics theorist Elizabeth El Refaie refers to this process of engaging with one's own identity through multiple self-portraits as "pictorial embodiment" (Refaie 2012, 51). At the level of form, in order to convey the rodent's movement, the author replicates the image of her rodent persona emerging out of the cage thrice, thereby overcoming the static nature of the comics page.

Elsewhere, Steinberg elaborates on the deeply depersonalising treatment procedures in the clinic, which rob her dignity and selfhood, thereby confirming her *gunea pig* predicament. The author clarifies that "every morning I was at the clinic at 6.45 for bloods and ultrasound". The splash page pictures a miserable-looking protagonist sitting on the examination table in the clinic with her bottom exposed, waiting for a transvaginal ultrasound.[2] Strikingly, although the scene is set in the clinic, no medical staff are seen around the protagonist. Instead, their presence is metonymically symbolised by a transducer,[3] which is directed towards the protagonist's exposed vagina, and also by the prober's commanding voice: "Empty your bladder! Take off everything below the waist. Cover yourself with a paper sheet." The final command of the prober is given in a yellow speech bubble: "Lie back and relax." With a tinge of sarcasm and black humour, Steinberg repeats the instructor's final command: "LIE BACK AND RELAX". Interestingly, the prober's final instruction is depicted in large fonts to foreground its ironic nature. At another level, the commanding nature of the prober's instructions, illustrated by the imperative sentences he utters, suggests the power dynamics at work during the examination. Here, Steinberg deploys the technique of repetition ("Lie back and relax"), as in the previous page ("guinea pig"), in order to create an echoing effect to help her reinforce the image/idea more effectively. The apathetic and authoritarian voice of the prober coupled with the intrusive and embarrassing nature of the ensuing medical procedure encapsulates the predicament of the protagonist in the clinic: a docile female body under a pervasive yet unseen, hence hegemonic, medical authority, subjected to a penetrative and intrusive medical gaze. The relegation of the protagonist's identity to that of a passive medicalised body under the clinical/technological gaze is yet another illustration of "the ultimate aim of western medicine as regards the bodily interior: to read that interior without interference from the subject" (Shaw 2012, 126).

Continuing to depict her harrowing medical encounter, Steinberg visualises herself undergoing a vaginal examination on the next splash page. Again, the transducer is the only marker of the presence of the prober, who is otherwise not visible on the page. The author describes the tormenting nature of her experience: "My feet in stirrups I spied the dreaded vaginal probe". Steinberg's deployment of the phrase "dreaded vaginal probe" (with the latter half of the phrase in bold) to describe the trauma that the examination engenders in the patient attests to the intrusive nature of medical tools in the context of infertility care. The image of the protagonist frightfully "spying" the "dreaded" transducer (probe) penetrating her vagina is deeply unsettling. The following splash page illustrates the impact of such an invasive and intrusive procedure on the protagonist. Unlike the previous pages, the protagonist is depicted on the page as a female dummy undergoing an ultrasound, which is suggestive of the objectifying and dehumanising nature of her clinical experience (see Figure 4.2). The dummy is depicted as lying with its legs spread and bottom exposed as a giant transducer is directed towards its vagina. Signifying the vulnerable nature of her existence, the dummy is depicted as enveloped by a reddish aura. In order to suggest the alienation and the loss of bodily integrity and personhood that the dummy-like experience engenders in her, Steinberg draws her half-face on the page's margin with her eye half-obliterated. The image conveys how the medical encounter has not only obliterated the protagonist's bodily integrity but also made her agency and subjectivity marginal. Further, illustrating the hastiness in which she was made to undergo the medical procedures, the author laments, "All before 7:00 am".

In fact, invasive medical procedures such as transvaginal ultrasound cause severe disorientation for many women. Some of them even describe their experience in terms of rape. For instance, in an interview with the Huffington Post, Marianne Keith narrates her traumatic encounter with a transvaginal ultrasound: "It felt like I was being raped … Like somebody was intentionally hurting me" (as quoted in Bassett 2013). Keith laments how, after such a procedure, she continues to experience "nightmares about being trapped" (as quoted in Bassett 2013). Clarifying that medical procedures such as transvaginal ultrasound have always been invasive for women irrespective of the context, Keith argues that "even if it's done the way that it should be done, it's so intrusive" (as quoted in Bassett 2013).

Steinberg's moving account of undergoing intrusive medical procedures in an apathetic fertility centre bears striking parallels to the

80 *The infertile body in the clinic*

Figure 4.2 Emily Steinberg, *Broken Eggs* (Cleaver, 2014). n.p.

depiction of estranging medical examinations in Jenell Johnson's graphic memoir on infertility, *Present/Perfect* (2018). While Steinberg pictures transvaginal ultrasound as invasive and debilitating, Johnson elaborates on the turmoil that similar procedures such as a sonohysterogram[4] and a hysteroscopy[5] engendered in her. Referring to her prolonged encounter with such procedures, Johnson describes her experience as follows: "We went through dozens of tests to try and figure out what was going on. Some hurt. Many were awkward and embarrassing" (102). Accordingly, the author depicts her tormenting experience with a sonohysterogram and a hysteroscopy in a couple of panels. The first panel depicts Johnson's reaction while undergoing the sonohysterogram, and she describes the procedure as follows: "Saline fills your uterus" (102). The panel depicts the protagonist's face as she squeezes her eyes shut and clenches her jaw, signifying the disgust and hurt she experiences. Ironically, the prober, who is seen nowhere in the panel, cautions the protagonist: "This might pinch a little" (102).

In the subsequent panel, Johnson narrates her encounter with the hysteroscopy: "A camera is sneaked through the cervix to get a peek at the uterus" (102). Referring to the medical negligence that aggravates her pain during the hysteroscopy, the author laments, "I had two [hysteroscopies], one while under general-ish anaesthesia – with a bonus polypectomy for a polyp that turned out not to exist. Oh, and a biopsy for good measure. I was wide awake during the second" (102). Here, it is evident that the protagonist was mistreated, as she was not given proper anaesthesia ("general-ish anaesthesia") and also was forced to undergo a surgical procedure (polypectomy) for a polyp that never existed. To convey the physical pain and the mental agony while undergoing such examinations, Johnson anthropomorphises her uterus. Having undergone hurtful medical examinations, a visibly distraught uterus moans, "Actually, I prefer listening to the cramps" (102), suggesting that the medical examination was more messy and painful than menstrual cramps. Here, the narrative draws the readers' attention to how women's bodies are parsed and disembodied into various parts in order to materially scrutinise and assess them. To quote Johnson herself, "I've never felt more like a body than I did while undergoing fertility treatment" (Johnson 2018, 2).

Both Steinberg's and Johnson's harrowing accounts of undergoing hurtful and intrusive medical procedures, such as a transvaginal ultrasound, sonohysterogram, and hysteroscopy, underscore the predicament of women in an increasingly technologised infertility care. These authors illustrate how they are doubly victimised, not only through the apathetic attitude of the medical professionals but also through the penetrative gaze of medical technology. In a sense, it is the invasive gaze of medical technology that aggravates their plight as patients. Further, the telling absence of medical professionals and their interventions in scenes where the authors' docile bodies are depicted as under technological gaze signifies how in medicine, "technology has come to be viewed as an autonomous process, having a life of its own which proceeds automatically, and almost naturally, along a singular path" (Noble 1984, x). Such scenes in both the narratives illustrate how human touch and empathy in a clinical setting are replaced by machines and technology. Existential critics of medicine, such as Martin Heidegger, have critiqued this technologisation of medicine by arguing that medicine's deployment of technology on patients should "not be identical to enforcing a 'framework' of technology on him or her, a new way of defining, shaping, and producing health and life under the reign of medical science" (Svenaeus 2018, 133). In a similar vein, commenting on X-ray as an example of medical imagining technologies' dehumanising gaze, Lisa Cartwright describes it as "an extreme example of a technique that renders its viewing subject an object of a pervasive disciplinary gaze – a truly radiant gaze – that threatens to perform a quite literal disintegration of the body" (108). At another level, the penetrative and invasive nature of these instruments and procedures manifests the mentality, values, objectives, and ideas of their makers, since "they are designed, developed, named and utilised by exclusive communities of medical and scientific professionals who are nearly always men" (Steinberg 1990, 74–75). As such, these technological apparatuses reveal the inherent misogyny of a patriarchal medical system. Against such a background, both the narratives attempt a critique of medical-scientific technology by illustrating how technological apparatuses and procedures in infertility care "constitute a structural language through which power is expressed in both material and social practices" (Steinberg 1990, 75).

Broken Eggs and *Present/Perfect* also elaborate on a series of other "mind-numbingly complex" (Steinberg) tests and procedures (such as intrauterine insemination (IUI), Clomid, and IVF) through which women's body parts and bodily processes are made available to the medical practitioners to experiment, excise, and manipulate. While Johnson succinctly depicts her predicament with a bloodstained short panel that details the hormonal treatments she underwent ("AMH, TSH ETC ETC.", 102), Steinberg laments the same: "a profusion of shots and hormones to stimulate some action in my lame ass ovaries." This administration of hormones, in particular, to make the patient "superovulate" during the treatment process invariably affects "not only the balance of her entire endocrine (hormone) system, but *all* organs and tissues that constitute her body" (Steinberg 1990, 80). Such procedures also cause abdominal discomfort, visual blurring, and hot flushes in women (Anderson 1987). Evidently, there is a singular lack of concern among medical practitioners for the hazards of hormone administration in women, as they focus narrowly on "their intention to control women's ovulation and induce them to produce many eggs, and on the disembodied objects of their intention, 'the' (women's) eggs, ovaries, and ovulation" (Steinberg 1990, 80). Illustrating this medical injustice, Johnson comments elsewhere: "The whole point of the hormones was to make me into a walking, talking, egg sac. My belly swelled so fast that I got stretch marks. I still have them" (105). Here, women are reduced to objects of medical manipulation, compromising their health and well-being. In essence, *Broken Eggs* and *Present/Perfect* illustrate how the methods and practices of infertility could be characterised as what

Ann Dally describes as macho: "aggressive, penetrative and sometimes ruthless" (Dally 2001, 12).

"Der straightener Herr Doktor": *The Facts of Life* and *Good Eggs*

Highlighting similar issues surrounding women's estranging encounter with fertility care, Paula Knight, in her autopathography on infertility, *The Facts of Life* (2017), portrays her embarrassing experience during a cervical screening. The author illustrates how she was treated casually by the nurse while her private parts were needlessly exposed for a considerably long time, making the screening an embarrassing and discomforting experience for her. The nurse, who rudely responds to the protagonist's queries regarding pregnancy and fertility by accusing her of delaying childbirth ("At your age, you haven't got time to waste 'thinking'" [83]), also gives her "spurious advice" that "the Pill would help preserve your eggs" (83). The nurse's misleading advice makes the author wonder, "What? It seems a bit odd to go on the Pill just as I'm thinking of trying to get pregnant!" (83). Snubbing the protagonist for her confusion, the nurse accusingly declares to her, "Fertility drops off pretty steeply after thirty-five" (84). Continuing her snide attitude regarding the protagonist's advanced age and the possible difficulty of getting pregnant, the nurse abruptly asks her to remove her clothes for screening: "Pop your bottom things off" (84). The next panel shows the protagonist, half-naked, sitting on the examination table. Interestingly, the nurse is not seen in the panel; instead, a surgical light is placed before the protagonist, focusing its glare on her naked vagina. In the nurse's absence, the protagonist is pictured as appraising the surgical light about her readiness for the screening ("Ready!").

Continuing her veiled attack on the technologisation/industrialisation of medicine, which replaces human interactions with intrusive and dehumanising equipment and medical tools, Knight illustrates in the next panel a huge vaginal speculum,[6] which is pictorially likened to a quacking duck ("quack-quack") (84). Here, referring to the intrusive nature of such medical tools, the author observes, "You never see where they produce speculums from – they just sort of appear" (85). The subsequent panels depict the protagonist being subjected to cervical screening, with the lower part of her body fully naked. The protagonist is asked to spread her legs, while the nurse's gaze is fixed on her vagina, which is illuminated by the surgical light. Surprisingly, the nurse's phone rings, and she leaves the room to attend the call, mumbling, "Just got to get that" (84). While the nurse is on her call, the protagonist is left exposed in the room, with her legs spread, under the glare of the surgical light. The author comments on her predicament: "It felt as if the nurse was on the phone for ages" (85). In fact, the author's comment on the invasiveness of the vaginal speculum is significant, since it is one of the first medical "instruments that have played a dramatic and controversial role in the history of women's health and that have placed women under the watchful eyes of others" (Sandelowski 2000, 73). Moreover, as Margarete Sandelowski (2000) observes, for women, a vaginal speculum has long meant "a kind of scrutiny and intrusion they have found aversive and have feared" (73). Again, this medical tool "signified the growing belief in clinical practice that to see was increasingly to know and that this kind of knowing was inextricably linked to power" (80).

Using the formal potency of the comics medium, Knight illustrates the traumatising nature of her *exposed* existence. The two adjacent panels portray the protagonist's naked lower body under the glare of the surgical light (see Figure 4.3). Each panel carries each of the protagonist's spread legs, with her limbs joining at the space between the two panels. Put differently, her legs are separated by the panels, and her vagina is trapped in the gutter. Again, the gutter is enlarged in the form of a womb, suggesting how her entire reproductive apparatus is caught in the gutter. Knight's creative use of the gutter to illustrate her predicament in the clinic draws special significance, since the gutter is the liminal space in a comics page where multiple meanings could be produced/performed. Unlike the comics panel, where the possible generation of meaning is anchored or "remote-controlled" (to use Roland Barthes terms) by the authorial intent, the gutter is the relatively neutral space that allows the reader multiple interpretive possibilities. The gutter also serves as a space of ambiguity, as the meanings produced in the gutter are not predetermined but varied. To quote Scott McCloud (1994), "the gutter plays host to much of the magic and mystery that are at the very heart of comics" (66). The authority of the author is challenged, and the reader's interpretive eye determines meanings in the gutter. Similarly, the clinic becomes a gutter-like space where the patient is deprived of her authority over her reproductive body, as it is subjected to the medical gaze to be interpreted and ascribed meanings.

Thus, Knight's picturing of her reproductive apparatus in the gutter conveys not only her uncertainty regarding her reproductive capacity but also the liminal nature of her existence under the medical/technological gaze. Further, each of the two panels depicts the author with her bottom fully exposed before the surgical light, pleading in vain, "Er…?" "…excuse me?" (Knight 2017, 85). Ironically, a board placed in

The infertile body in the clinic 85

Figure 4.3 Paula Knight, *The Facts of Life* (Myriad, 2017), 85.

front of the examination room reads, "PLEASE RESPECT PATIENT DIGNITY" (85). In sum, Knight's narrative illustrates the unsympathetic manner in which the medical establishment treats the infertile female body, as it is exposed, shamed, and made vulnerable.

Echoing similar sentiments, Phoebe Potts' graphic pathography on infertility, *Good Eggs* (2010), illustrates her traumatising experience in the clinic while undergoing embryo transfer. The author pictures herself lying on the examination table with her legs parted and attached to the stirrups as the male doctor along with two nurses direct their gaze towards her fully exposed vagina. Upon observing that the protagonist's "uterus is severely tipped" (147), the doctor asks his assistant to get him a uterus straightener. The protagonist, who is visibly upset (signified by her horrified-looking visage), incessantly thumps her husband who is standing beside her. Taking an ominous turn, the next panel pictures a scary man (with a large body, wearing a monkey cap) appearing in the room carrying a huge and imposing straightener. The intimidating appearance of the man (who is ostensibly a nurse) with a monkey-cap that covers his face (making only his eyes visible), and the huge straightener, scares the protagonist and her husband, who covers her eyes with his hands. The man announces in German, "Der straightener Herr Doktor" (The straightener, Mr Doctor) (148).

Again, while the protagonist looks perplexed (indicated by the thought balloon that carries a question mark glyph), the doctor thanks the nurse ("Thank you, nurse") for bringing him the straightener as the nurse disappears from the scene. The subsequent short panel shows the hurt and horror that the protagonist experiences while the doctor attaches the straightener to her cervix. While the straightener facilitates the doctor's task (he casually comments after attaching the cervix, "That's better"), the experience causes severe harm to the protagonist, as she is pictured as jumping up from the examination table, thumping her husband's hand. Further, to accentuate the magnitude of her suffering, Potts adopts a cartoony style, drawing her head in an exaggerated form, as she screams indistinctly with sweat drops scattering from her head.

In the next borderless panel, commenting on her experience, the author criticises sarcastically not only the doctor for his inhuman attitude but also the whole system, which aggravates her predicament with "medieval" medical tools: "So there I am, legs open in the air, medieval uterus straightener attached to my cervix, a catheter up my hey-nonny-nonny, my bladder full to bursting and the doctor has the nerve to say: 'You've got to relax'" (148). Deploying black humour, the author vents her frustration towards the doctor by telling her husband, "I'm gonna pee in his face" (148). The author's husband, who has been a mute spectator to her harrowing experience, trivialises her angry outburst with a smile thus: "That's my girl" (148). Evidently, his response is symptomatic of the incapability of men in general of empathising with the lived realities of suffering that their female partners undergo in an overtly patriarchal and abusive system of care. In essence, both Knight and Potts in their respective memoirs portray their uncomfortable experience of abusive infertility care. The memoirists not only lament the apathy of the medical professionals, whose callous attitude causes mental and physical harm to the patients, but also foreground the intrusive nature of medical tools that aggravate their suffering.

Conclusion

Feminist critics of medicalisation argue that healthcare institutions and practices are profoundly patriarchal and that discourses of medicine contribute to the sexist ideology. Feminist scholars identify obstetrics, gynaecology, and reproductive medicine as one such domain where the medical subjectification of women is clearly revealed. Arguing that the medicalisation of women's reproduction reinforces patriarchal control over women's bodies, feminists lament medicine's treatment of pregnant bodies as reproducing machines. Under medical surveillance, women's bodies are exposed, penetrated, and hence made vulnerable. Further, the history of reproductive medicine reveals its inherent misogyny, as it demonises infertile women as a "deviant" category. Contemporary feminist critique of reproductive medicine is centred primarily on the technological intrusion of women's bodies made possible by ARTs. Feminists note that ARTs, under the guise of according women reproductive choice, make their reproductive lives available for medical manipulation.

In this context, graphic pathographies on female infertility such as Potts' *Good Eggs*, Steinberg's *Broken Eggs*, Knight's *The Facts of Life*, and Johnson's *Present/Perfect* gain significance, as these narratives foreground the authors' dehumanising and estranging encounters in the infertility clinic. Utilising comics' affordances, these graphic texts accentuate the memoirists' psychological turmoil of undergoing treatment in a system of care that is unsympathetic and intrusive. While Steinberg's narrative attempts a forthright critique of infertility care, which treats her like a "fertility guinea pig", Johnson's short comic explores the ontology of hurt and estrangement that the treatments engender in the author. Parallels could be found in *Broken Eggs* and *Present/Perfect*, as both narratives explore nuanced issues concerning infertility care, such as the technological invasion of women's bodies and medical apathy. Illustrating, as it were, comics' and graphic medicine's subversive potential, Steinberg, in particular, exposes the patriarchal impulses that guide medical attitudes and treatment procedures. In a similar vein, Potts and Knight, in their respective memoirs, portray their experiences of hurt, shame, and estrangement. Additionally, Steinberg's and Johnson's picturing of ART as depersonalising and hurtful alongside Potts' and Knight's depiction of medical tools as instruments of intrusion signify how the mechanisation and technologisation of medicine have impacted women adversely, making them more vulnerable to surveillance and invasion. In essence, by narrativising their subjective realities of undergoing infertility treatment, these authors lend a voice to the alienating experiences of women whose bodies and lives are exposed, excised, and manipulated by an authoritarian and misogynistic system of care.

Notes

1. ARTs include techniques and procedures such as in vitro fertilisation (IVF) and embryo transfer (ET) that are deployed in the treatment of infertility and related issues.
2. A transvaginal ultrasound is a procedure used to examine the internal organs in the female pelvic region. The method "involves the insertion of the transducer into the vagina to produce incredibly detailed images of the organs" (Eske 2018).
3. An ultrasound transducer is a device used to make pictures of different parts of the body. The image created using the transducer is called a sonogram.
4. A sonohysterogram is "an imaging study of the uterus. Doctors insert fluid into the uterus via the cervix to examine the uterine lining" (Nall 2019).
5. A hysteroscopy is used in the diagnosis and treatment of issues in the uterus or womb. During the procedure, a camera is "inserted into the uterus via the vagina. The camera has a light on the end and is called a hysteroscope" (Barrell 2017).
6. A vaginal speculum is an instrument used in gynaecological examinations in order to widen the vaginal opening so that the cervix is easily visible.

Acknowledgements

This chapter is derived in part from an article published in *Women's Studies* on 22 July 2020 copyright Taylor & Francis, available online: www.tandfonline.com/10.1080/00497878.2020.1785879

References

Anderson, Mary. 1987. *Infertility: A Guide for the Anxious Couple*. London: Faber & Faber.

Barrell, Amanda. 2017. "What you should Know about Hysteroscopy." *Medical News Today,* 28 December. www.medicalnewstoday.com/articles/320451.php. Accessed 15 July 2019.

Bassett, Laura. 2013. "Woman Sues over Transvaginal Ultrasound: 'It Felt Like I was Being Raped.'" *Huffington Post*, 11 September. www.huffingtonpost.com.au/2013/09/11/transvaginal-ultrasound-lawsuit_n_3907422.html. Accessed 25 May 2019.

Dally, Ann. 2001. "Women and Macho Medicine." In *Women and Modern Medicine*, ed. Lawrence I. Conrad and Anne Hardy. Leiden: Brill. doi: https://doi.org/10.1163/9789004333390_002.
Daly, Mary. 1979. *Gyn/Ecology: The Metaethics of Radical Feminism*. London: Women's Press.
Davis, Gayle, and Tracey Loughran. 2017. "Introduction: Situating Infertility in Medicine." In *The Palgrave Handbook of Infertility in History*, ed. Gayle Davis and Tracey Loughran, 265–271. London: Palgrave Macmillan.
Davis-Floyd, Robbie. 1992. *Birth as an American Rite of Passage*. Berkeley, CA: University of California Press.
Ehrenreich, Barbara, and Deirdre English. 1974. *Complaints and Disorders: The Sexual Politics of Sickness*. London: Compendium.
Eske, Jamie. 2018. "What to Know about Transvaginal Ultrasounds." *Medical News Today*, 11 September. www.medicalnewstoday.com/articles/323041.php. Accessed 6 May 2019.
Greil, Arthur L. 2002. "Infertile Bodies: Medicalisation, Metaphor, and Agency." In *Infertility around the Globe: New Thinking on Childlessness, Gender, and Reproductive Technologies*, ed. Marcia C. Inhorn and Frank Van Balen, 101–118. Berkeley: University of California Press.
Johnson, Jenell. 2018. "Introduction." In *Graphic Reproduction: A Comics Anthology*, ed. Jenell Johnson, 1–16. University Park: Pennsylvania State University Press.
Johnson, Jenell. 2018. "Present/Perfect." In *Graphic Reproduction: A Comics Anthology*, ed. Jenell Johnson, 99–114. University Park: Pennsylvania State University Press.
Knight, Paula. 2017. *The Facts of Life*. Oxford: Myriad.
Lam, Carle. 2015. *New Reproductive Technologies and Disembodiment: Feminist and Material Resolutions*. Farnham: Ashgate.
Lupton, Deborah. 1997. "Foucault and the Medicalisation Critique." In *Foucault, Health and Medicine*, ed. Alan Petersen and Robin Bunton, 94–110. London: Routledge.
Martin, Emily. 2001. *The Woman in the Body: A Cultural Analysis of Reproduction*. Boston, MA: Beacon Press.
McCloud, Scott. 1994. *Understanding Comics*. New York: Harper Perennial.
Nall, Rachel. 2019. "Sonohysterogram: What to Expect." Healthline,18 June. www.healthline.com/health/womens-health/sonohysterogram". Accessed 15 July 2019.
Noble, David. 1984. *The Forces of Production*. New York: Knopf.
Potts, Phoebe. 2010. *Good Eggs: A Memoir*. New York: Harper Collins.
Refaie, Elisabeth El. 2012. *Autobiographical Comics: Life Writing in Pictures*. Jackson, MS: University Press of Mississippi.
Sandelowski, Margarete. 2000. "'This Most Dangerous Instrument': Propriety, Power, and the Vaginal Speculum." *JOGNN* 29(1): 73–82. doi: 10.1111/j.1552-6909.2000.tb02759.x

Shaw, Jennifer. 2012. "*The Birth of the Clinic* and the Advent of Reproduction: Pregnancy, Pathology and the Medical Gaze in Modernity." *Body and Society* 18(2): 110–138.

Spallone, Patricia. 1989. *Beyond Conception: The New Politics of Reproduction*. Basingstoke: Macmillan Education Ltd.

Steinberg, Deborah Lynn. 1990. "The Depersonalisation of Women through the Administration of 'In Vitro Fertilisation.'" In *The New Reproductive Technologies*, ed. Maureen McNeil, Ian Varcoe, and Steven Yearley, 74–122. London: Macmillan Press.

Steinberg, Emily. 2014. "Broken Eggs." *Cleaver*, 10 September. www.cleavermagazine.com/broken-eggs-by-emily-steinberg/". Accessed 15 July 2019.

Svenaeus, Fredrik. 2018. "Heidegger's Philosophy of Technology and the Perils of Medicalization." In *Existential Medicine: Essays on Health and Illness*, ed. Kevin Aho, 131–44. London: Rowman & Littlefield International.

5 Traversing infertility
Endurance and alternatives

Introduction

As a gendered and stigmatised health predicament, female infertility engenders intense psychic turmoil in the sufferers. Infertile women often internalise pronatal cultural scripts and the social expectations of the female gender, perceiving themselves as an inadequate and abnormal category. Oscillating between multiple negative affective states, the infertile subjects are alienated not only from their familiar socio-cultural landscapes but also from their idealised notions of self-identity. Traversing the challenges of infertility, therefore, demands tremendous effort from the sufferers who are expected to refashion their identities to the practical and affective challenges of childlessness. In such a context, the concept of resilience through which the sufferers positively adapt to their infertile subjectivity serves as an adequate method of coping. This chapter examines the concept of resilience and coping in the framework of female infertility. The chapter close reads two graphic medicine narratives, Phoebe Potts' *Good Eggs*, and Paula Knight's *The Facts of Life*, to illustrate how the authors successfully navigate the psychic challenges of infertility through a positive coping practice. The chapter specifically foregrounds the ways in which the memoirists, as resilient subjects, draw on their values and existential goals to find meaning and purpose in existence, overcoming the psychic dilemmas of infertility.

Resilience, coping, and infertile subjectivity

Experience of infertility is often chaotic and leaves on the sufferer a permanent ontological scar that mediates her everyday realities. As such, the crisis of infertility is experienced "not simply as the physical dysfunction of the mechanistic body, but as the disorder of the body,

DOI: 10.4324/9781003028628-6

self and world" (Toombs 1988, 202). The condition engenders in the suffering subject complex affective states: grief and depression, anger, guilt, shock or denial, and anxiety (Schetter and Lobel 1991, 30). These emotions are also exacerbated by the sense of loss of control over the present and the future (33). The physical and psychological ordeals of infertility disrupt women's self-identity in multiple ways. Specifically, childless women "go through a process of 'taking on' an identity of 'self' as infertile" (Roudsari et al. 2014, 114). Again, the gendered realities of childlessness alienate the subject from her idealised imaginings of the self and affect her self-esteem through a sense of failure, loss, and inadequacy. The social stigma surrounding the condition engenders self-doubt and self-loathing in the subject.

The infertile women internalise the social expectations of the female gender, which entwine femininity with motherhood, and they perceive themselves as an "abnormal female". Here, the subject experiences what Sartre describes as the third order of intersubjectivity: "I exist for myself as a body known by the other" (Sartre 2003, 375). As such, the sufferers struggle to "reconcile their opposing identities of self, views of the world, and images of an anticipated future" (McCarthy 2008, 320). Worse still, women's struggles with infertility are compounded by fertility treatments which often last for several years, lacking desired outcomes. In fact, the culmination of unsuccessful fertility treatments exacts tremendous psychic toll, and "triggers a renewed cycle of grieving and distress" in the sufferers (Harvard Medical School 2009).

As a health condition that affects the subject's self-identity in complex ways, it is evident that an attempt to cope with infertility is essentially "an experience of intense suffering coupled with an introspective effort to rediscover a sense of self and a feeling of balance, purpose, and meaning in their lives" (McCarthy 2008, 320). In other words, infertility requires from the sufferers "serious effort and continuous work to adapt practically to its limitations and to adjust psychologically to the pain, restricted horizons, and frustration it brings" (Carel 2016, 3). Psychologically speaking, the concept of resilience offers an adequate method of navigating the crisis of childlessness. In simple terms, resilience involves an "ability to bend but not break, bounce back, and perhaps even grow in the face of adverse life experiences" (Southwick et al. 2014, 2). Resilience enables the subject to endure the trauma and suffering that an adversity creates and successfully overcome its affective challenges. Put differently, the mechanism of resilience includes a refashioning of "self that includes a conscious effort to move forward" (2014, 3). The notion of moving forward is a significant component of resilience since the subject's successful navigation of the crisis inevitably involves a sense of the future in positive terms. An awareness that harnessing "resources toward securing a better future matter more than the turmoil and traumas of the past" (2014, 6) is central to the mechanism of resilience. A sense of hope amid chaos, a recognition that "life does indeed make sense, despite chaos, brutality, stress, worry, or despair" (2014, 6), enables the resilient individual to create meaning and purpose in suffering. The sufferer "draws on his or her beliefs (e.g., religious, spiritual, or beliefs about justice), values (e.g., 'mattering'), and existential goals (e.g., purpose in life or guiding principles) to motivate and sustain coping and well-being" (Folkman 2008, 7). In essence, this sense of "hope or 'meaning-making' is the essence of a cultural perspective on resilience" (2008, 6).

In the context of coping with infertility, the process of meaning-making happens at different levels. The process involves the sufferer developing her life story, choosing pivotal events and themes from her life, which validate her self-identity. The subject draws resources from the past, filters memories, and chooses elements that enable her to "steer a course into the future" (Becker 1997, 215). As such, the subject turns to inner resources for navigating the crisis of childlessness. Further, a positive refashioning of the self which combines the subject's pre-crisis identity and the new aspects of life post-crisis allows the subject to create new meanings and hopes for her existence notwithstanding her infertile subjectivity (245). Letting go of the hope to conceive a child is an essential component in navigating the ordeals of infertility. This involves the sufferer not only acknowledging and mourning the predicament of infertility but also altering her life-perspectives. As Gay Becker observes, "[p]art of letting go lies in rethinking what generativity means" (242). Rejecting the restrictive conceptualisation of generativity as procreation, the subject should embrace a broader vision which perceives generativity through other forms of creation and nurturing, transcending the biological (242). Finally, successful coping with infertility includes a process of self-acceptance. The sufferers destigmatise their infertile identity by rejecting "the sense of stigma they formerly associated with their infertility" (247–248). In essence, navigating the predicament of infertility requires the sufferers to not only re-examine the philosophy of life and existence but also adapt to its limitations and challenges. Put differently, infertility "involves both minor and major losses requiring different coping strategies to adjust successfully, adapt, and preserve emotional balance regardless of the ultimate outcome" (Roudsari et al. 2014, 114).

Spiritual and creative coping in *Good Eggs*

Potts' memoir concludes when the protagonist decides to stop fertility treatments after "five attempts at invitro fertilisation, five miscarriages and four years of every fertility procedure imaginable including acupuncture and yoga" (Potts 2011). The concluding part of *Good Eggs* depicts the author's mental crisis when her long and tedious journey through fertility treatments, or the "infertility odyssey" (Potts 2011) as she calls it, comes to an end. In the memoir, the author and her partner receive a call from the doctor informing them that their frozen embryo treatment has failed to produce the desired result (Potts 2010, 235). The awful and disruptive impact of the news on the couple is deftly conveyed by the author as the shockwave-like borders of the doctor's speech balloons break the panel borders and cross the hyperframe (235).

Despite the doctor's suggestion that they could continue the treatment, since there are "some embryos frozen – a thaw cycle is very straightforward, with less drugs – and no egg retrieval" (Potts 2010, 235), the protagonist decides to discontinue fertility treatments, stating that they have done everything their "insurance will approve" (235). Illustrating the mental agony she had to experience while undergoing treatment, Potts observes thus: "this process has been like structured insanity. I think I'm relieved it's over – I would never have had the resolve to end it myself" (235). In retrospect, the couple laments that the fertility treatment has put them "on a long and expensive road, full of hope and heartbreak" (236). The subsequent panel captures the protagonist with her husband in half-embrace, assuring each other that they "really tried", suggesting their mutual love and support (236).

Taking the narrative forward, one of the short panels depicts the protagonist as lying down on the couch with her partner, presumably trying an emotional recovery from the treatment failure. Strangely, a "THUMPA THUMP" sound from the background leaves the couple astonished, and an elephant emerges in the background (Potts 2010, 237). The author recognises "the elephant in the room" as adoption, observing that adoption is another "long and expensive road" (237). The author's metaphorical treatment of adoption as "the elephant in the room" idiomatically connotes that adoption is an issue they did not wish to address. Interestingly, the harness on the elephant's back carries the inscription "PLAN B" (237). Moreover, the animal is depicted as an imposing presence, almost occupying one-third of the panel, inviting the scared-looking couple to pursue adoption. The panel signifies how adoption is perceived as an inevitable second choice for infertile couples as they are expected to parent a foster-child in the absence of a biological one.

The protagonist declines the elephant's invitation thus: "[w]e are not ready to talk about it yet! We've got to MOURN for chrissake!" (Potts 2010, 237). The elephant, as it moves towards the kitchen, is depicted as unbothered by the response, stating: "[n]o problem – I'm not going anywhere!" (237). The following splash page pictures the elephant in the kitchen, calmly swallowing every food item as the couple watches in desperation in the background (238), signifying how adoption can exhaust the couple financially. Intriguingly, the elephant advises the protagonist on the merits of adoption and the need to proceed to it at the earliest thus: "[w]hen you guys are ready you should know that China has a 3 year waiting list for a girl. Guatemala & Vietnam have been closed for adoption for now" (238). Indicating how the author is troubled by the thoughts of adoption, symbolised by the elephant, she observes: "[b]ut adoption has the highest success rate of getting folks like us a baby. Which means we can raise a family. We will become parents. Which by all accounts is another journey, long, expensive" (238). Again, the last page of the main text of the narrative carries the image of an empty hummus box, and a spilled snack pack with the caption, "full of hope … and heartbreak" (239), signifying how emotionally draining and financially exhausting adoption can be for the couple.

Notably, *Good Eggs*' Afterword depicts how the author positively copes with her infertile subjectivity, drawing sustenance from her Jewish ancestry, spirituality, and artistic creativity. Although the unsuccessful culmination of years of fertility treatments leaves the protagonist in limbo, Potts approaches her predicament in philosophical terms. The author pictures herself as a young girl playing hide and seek with her dog in the field. According to Potts, they played the game in such a way that she "would fall flat on the ground in the high grass" (Potts 2010, 243) and the dog would home in on the author's scent, making "smaller and tighter circles" around her. Tellingly, the author deploys the game metaphor of the dog and her childhood persona to illustrate that she never thought of her "life as on a straight trajectory, always moving forward" (245). Potts clarifies thus: "[i]nstead I would compare myself to the dog: each path I took, each choice I made circled me in on my target" (245). Here, the author is drawing on her memory of a simple childhood experience to attribute positive meanings to her present reality. The memoirist compares herself to her pet dog and approaches her long and arduous journey of infertility and every path and choice that she had made during the journey as rewarding. Potts means to suggest that her journey of infertility has enabled her to find new meanings and purpose in her present existence.

Continuing her attempts to overcome the existential dilemmas of her non-mother identity, Potts affirms her Hebrew ancestry. As such, the author uses a religious metaphor, drawing parallels between her journey of infertility and her Hebrew ancestors' voyage to the holy land "which took them 40 years" (Potts 2010, 245). Potts observes: "now I think I'm more like my Hebrew ancestors, meandering around in the wilderness … God wouldn't let them into the promised land until they had grown up. It was hard out there" (245). By likening her "infertility odyssey" to the Jews' journey in search of the holy land, Potts accords spiritual significance to her experience of childlessness. The author attempts a spiritual identification with her Hebrew ancestry, believing that her experience of infertility is predestined by God, as a journey towards her spiritual maturity. This spiritual perspective of her non-mother identity enables the author to find meaning and purpose in her struggles with infertility and its attendant challenges. Potts' invocation of her Jewish identity and her reliance on spirituality illustrate how infertile women can navigate the affective and existential challenges of infertility, adopting "a religious and spiritual meaning-making framework" (Roudsari et al. 2014, 119). As Roudsari et al. contend, "[u]sing religious and spiritual coping strategies may enhance self-empowerment of infertile women to find meaning and purpose in life, as their sense of personal wholeness is disrupted through infertility" (Roudsari et al. 2007, 145–146). Through a religious reappraisal of their predicament, infertile women not only attempt to come to terms with childlessness but also perceive infertility as a catalyst for their spiritual growth and transformation. Arguably, Potts' affirmation of her Jewish identity and her likening of her situation to that of her Hebrew ancestors demonstrate how the author uses her spiritual and religious beliefs as a source for successful coping.

Finally, Potts affirms the role of art and storytelling in the context of coping with her childlessness. In order to illustrate the soothing potential of storytelling, the author refers to Jews' biblical journey and their storytelling practices: "[t]hey suffered and they celebrated. And they accumulated materials for stories to make it through the long haul" (Potts 2010, 247). While narrating her ancestors' stories, Potts pictures herself on her drawing table, immersed in the act of creating her memoir (*Good Eggs*). Specifically, the image depicts the author drawing one of the pages of her memoir, making the narrative self-reflexive. Evidently, Potts' invocation of her ancestors' storytelling practices and picturing of herself creating the memoir illustrate the power of storytelling and creativity in the face of adversities. Here, the author implies that her creation of the memoir becomes another storytelling practice which enabled her to overcome the pain of childlessness. In fact, storytelling and artistic creativity has often been recognised as a powerful method of coping in the context of illness and suffering. As Sunwolf et al. observe, illness and its treatment

> challenge those who are affected to construct meanings that create a tolerable narrative for what appears to be inexplicable. In such a context, storytelling is viewed as a form of communication that can help people to successfully cope with and reframe illnesses and, thereby, create the paradoxical possibility of being "successfully ill."
> (Sunwolf et al. 2005, 237–238)

In other words, artistic expression enables the ill to "create congruence between their affective states and their conceptual sense making" (Yorks and Kasl 2006, 53).

In an interview, Potts elaborates on her invocation of her Jewish ancestry and the importance of storytelling in coping with the crisis of infertility thus:

> Jews tell stories. So does everyone else. Jews tell stories as part of the Jewish practice to connect across time and space and to have something in common with each other and their ancestors. I do feel a need for a community of people who care about me, I need to care about other people, and I crave good storytelling. So that's why I invoke Torah in my book – I wanted to connect to something bigger than myself and remind myself (and my reader/viewer) that this isn't the end of the story.
> (as quoted in Venkatesan and Murali 2020, 13)

Evidently, Potts' gesture of translating her experience of infertility into a comic narrative becomes an aesthetic coping practice. The author creatively uses her artistic impulses and narrativises the predicament of infertility in comics form, thereby alleviating her psychic turmoil. In essence, Potts' memoir demonstrates how the author not only refashions her identity and perspectives in philosophical and spiritual terms but also draws sustenance from artistic creativity and storytelling practices to navigate infertility with resilience and fortitude.

Art, ecology, and alternative mothering practices in *The Facts of Life*

Arthur Frank in his memoir *At the Will of the Body: Reflections on Illness* conceptualises illness as "a dangerous opportunity" which helps the sufferer to reflect on life in philosophical terms. Emphasising the potential of the illness experience to change the sufferer's life-perspectives, Frank observes thus: "[i]llness takes away parts of your life, but in doing so it gives you the opportunity to choose the life you will lead, as opposed to living out the one you have simply accumulated over the years" (Frank 2002, n.p). Havi Carel, in a similar vein, accentuates the edifying role of illness when she argues that illness can be "a source of personal growth and learning" (Carel 2013, 345). The experience of illness enables the subject to develop a deeper self-understanding as it enlightens her emotionally and existentially (346). Theorising the positive outcomes of experience of illness, Carel argues that "illness could elicit creative personal and philosophical responses" (Carel 2007, 96). The sufferer's positive experience of illness is achieved through what Carel describes as "adaptability" and "creativity" (104). The idea that "illness induces adaptability and that adversity is the source of creative response to it" (104) serves as the foundational principle in theorising the positive and transformative impact of illness in the sufferers.

Knight's memoir *The Facts of Life* demonstrates how the author creatively adapts to her infertile identity. Adopting a resilient coping perspective, Knight accepts her experience of childlessness as an opportunity for personal growth and learning. In the memoir, Knight delineates how Polly, the fictional avatar of the author, decides to give up the hope of motherhood after undergoing three miscarriages. Polly's decision to discontinue the pursuit of parenthood is also due to the fact that trying ART treatments such as IVF might further debilitate her weak body. The concluding pages of the second part of the memoir depict Polly and her partner Jack reassuring each other that ceasing the pursuit of parenthood was the right decision for them (Knight 2017, 168).

Interestingly, the third part of the narrative opens with a splash page portraying the image of a seed sprouting, which is symbolic of the author's new sense of personal growth, hope, and rejuvenation. Nevertheless, Knight pictures her sense of despair, and moments of grief as she comes to terms with her infertile subjectivity. The succeeding page pictures Polly sending her unused pregnancy test to an art exhibition. Commenting on her gesture to donate the pregnancy test to the art exhibition, the author observes: "[h]anding it over represents the start of my grief, which coincided with this exhibition invitation" (Knight 2017, 234).

Further, Knight illustrates how she was plagued by the fact that she is unable to pass on to her children the "precious things" she inherited, such as her "gran's wedding ring", "the lion's tooth" her dad gifted her,

her "mum's pressed flowers, collected in 1954", among others. The protagonist is also tormented by the existential questions of death, legacy, and mortality: "[i]t's human to feel the need to leave some sort of legacy ... With no children, one must learn to accept the finality of death ... Without a child in my life between now ... and sometime later ... my mortality came into focus" (Knight 2017, 181, 182). Puzzled by the thought of a future without children, Polly also confronts her own insecurities regarding ageing: "[a]s an only-child adult with no children, the prospect of ageing seemed bleak" (182).

Notably, after navigating through a vexing grieving process, the protagonist not only comes to terms with her own predicament of childlessness but also illustrates how her experience of traversing infertility has brought about radical transformations in her individuality. Knight emphasises her resolve not to be dispirited by her non-mother identity: "I was determined to lead a life that was fulfilling. After all, people without children are free to do as they please" (Knight 2017, 189). Rejecting her own earlier concern that she wouldn't have a legacy or a link to the future since she was unable to beget a baby, Knight observes: "how you conduct your life while you are living ... is much more important than any 'thing' that you might leave behind" (188). Here, the author refashions her perspectives and priorities as an attempt to gracefully embrace her childless existence. Knight affirms that her earlier "expectations" of a happy and fulfilled life, which involved traditional expectations such as children, wealth, house, and a stable job, "were changing" (195). Alternatively, the author's changed perspective towards life is characterised by finding happiness and fulfilment through art and nature. In her attempt to positively cope with infertility, Knight envisions two alternatives to biological motherhood, which involve both the creative and nurturing aspects of parenting: the pursuit of art and the natural world.

Knight reaffirms her artistic identity and foregrounds the potential of artistic creativity as an alternative to biological mothering. The memoirist recognises the power of art to transcend time and hence to be a permanent link to the future: "I realised that it was still possible to have a connection to the future through what I do now" (Knight 2017,188). Illustrating this point, the protagonist is pictured as creating a picture book for children. In the subsequent borderless panel, a father is seen reading the picture book that Knight authored (evidenced by the author's name on the book's jacket cover) to his daughter. This image allows the memoirist to foreground the fact that procreation is not the only way to have a connection to the future, as the author could attain immortality through her artistic creativity.

100 *Traversing infertility*

Elsewhere, Knight affirms how her priority of biological motherhood was replaced by the pursuit of art over the course of time. The image visualises Polly blissfully sitting on a pile of sand falling from an hourglass, surrounded by painting pads, paint brushes, pastels, pencils, pens, paint bottles, and a guitar (see Figure 5.1). Interestingly, this

Figure 5.1 Paula Knight, *The Facts of Life* (Myriad, 2017), 214.

image depicts a resolution to Polly's crisis which the author portrayed in the second part of the memoir: in one of the splash pages, Knight shows Polly in two distinct identities, as a pregnant woman and as a visual artist. The two selves of the author are also separated by an hourglass. The image conveys the author's dilemma as she had to make an immediate choice between the two selves. The present image provides a resolution to the crisis when she embraces the creative facets of her personality after giving up the pursuit of motherhood. Commenting on her identification with her artistic self which was lying dormant during her efforts to conceive, Knight remarks: "[i]n time, a strong creative urge took hold, and that became my priority at the expense of other activities" (Knight 2017, 214).

Later, the author also illustrates how her interest and involvement in the natural world allowed her to find emotional fulfilment. Accordingly, Polly is pictured as happily devoting herself to planting trees, feeding and watching birds, and keeping bees. The author comments on her interest and involvement in the natural world as an alternative to biological motherhood: "[f]ulfilment could be found in ways other than having a baby ... I wouldn't miss out on fun just because we didn't have kids" (Knight 2017, 195). Elsewhere, Knight portrays how the protagonist was happy and thrilled after seeing the acorn seed that she kept in a pot sprout. The splash page depicts the sprouted acorn in the pot as surrounded by radiant rays which symbolise the sense of hope and renewal it brings to the protagonist (232). Evidently, nature and wildlife enable Knight to find hope and purpose in her life, thereby alleviating the pain of childlessness.

Similarly, the memoir's Prologue consists of a series of silent visuals of the author and her partner collecting, planting, and nurturing saplings in a vast and barren landscape (Knight 2017, 8–11). In the book's Afterword, the author clarifies the significance of these silent visuals. According to the author, she became involved with the National Forest's "Grow a Tree from a Seed" scheme. As part of this ecological initiative, Knight plants acorns in Poppy Wood in Derbyshire, thereby helping transform a barren land into a small forest (238). The author elucidates the significance of this initiative on her infertile subjectivity: "[a]fter being unable to grow life in my body, it felt restorative and hopeful to make a contribution towards new ecosystems and communities – to help regenerate what used to be a damaged and barren landscape" (238). Again, in a personal email interview, Knight clarifies how her gesture of planting acorns helped her create a "small connection to the future" (238). The author also observes that her involvement in ecological initiatives is more meaningful and rewarding (to herself and to the planet) than traditional mothering practices:

> I think having children can give people a sense of life after life, and, for me, planting the trees provided that same sense: Trees last longer than people and are more environmentally friendly because they gobble up CO_2 rather than creating it.
>
> (as quoted in Venkatesan and Murali 2020, 11)

Knight here attempts an oblique critique of overpopulation and its attendant environmental challenges. The author proposes ecological consciousness as an alternative to traditional forms of mothering, in the process illustrating how it is equally rewarding for the self and for the community. Knight's involvement in nature and wildlife as a distinct form of parenting illustrates how she attempts to "improvise and create new ways of compensating for a lost capacity", also demonstrating "the plasticity of behaviour and the human capacity to adjust to change" (Carel 2007, 106).

In essence, the memoir illustrates how Knight uses her experience of infertility to develop a deeper understanding of her own self, also redefining her priorities and choices in the process. The memoirist's identification with her artistic self and her devout involvement in ecological concerns signify the way her previous notions of motherhood and fulfilment are altered in creative ways. For Knight, childlessness becomes "a tool of self-discovery and a fundamental source of later self-development" (Moch 1989, 24). Knight's creative use of her artistic impulses and interest in the natural world as a method of finding meaning and hope in the face of infertility becomes a unique resilient coping practice. As Victor Frankl observes,

> We must never forget that we may also find meaning in life even when confronted with a hopeless situation, when facing a fate that cannot be changed. For what then matters is to bear witness to the uniquely human potential at its best, which is to transform a personal tragedy into a triumph, to turn one's predicament into a human achievement. When we are no longer able to change a situation ... we are challenged to change ourselves.
>
> (1985, 135)

Conclusion

An attempt to successfully cope with the predicament of infertility requires serious and continuous effort from the subjects. Psychologically speaking, the concept of resilience serves as an adequate coping practice in the context of infertility. As resilient individuals, infertile women refashion themselves and adapt to the limitations of childlessness. The mechanisms of resilience for overcoming the affective challenges of infertility involve a refashioning of the subject's identity. As such, harnessing emotional resources to move forward, infertile women develop a sense of hope amid chaos. Central to this endeavour is the process of "meaning-making" in which the resilient subject draws on her beliefs, values, and existential goals to create meaning and purpose in suffering. Such a coping practice enables the subject to not only navigate the crisis of infertility successfully but also to sustain her wellbeing.

Graphic memoirs on infertility such as Phoebe Potts' *Good Eggs* and Paula Knight's *The Facts of Life* illustrate how the authors overcome the affective challenges of childlessness through resilience methods and practices. After going through a brief period of grief and mourning, both the authors successfully attempt a refashioning of their identity, also drawing on their values and goals to find hope and meaning in life and existence. Both the artists recognise the significance of artistic creativity in their coping practice. While Potts approaches her infertility in spiritual and creative terms, Knight affirms the role of art and the natural world in coming to terms with her non-mother identity. *Good Eggs* reveals how Potts draws impetus from her Jewish faith and its storytelling practices (which inspire her to narrate her own story of infertility) and approaches her "infertility odyssey" in metaphysical terms. With a religious reappraisal of childlessness, Potts perceives her journey of infertility as a source of spiritual growth and transformation. Knight's narrative, on the other hand, attains special significance as it demonstrates the possibility of self-realisation and personal growth in the process of coping with infertility. With an affirmation of her artistic self and a renewed interest in nature and wildlife, Knight not only sublimates her infertile predicament but also refashions her identity and priorities in creative terms. Furthermore, Knight's creative adaptation to her infertile subjectivity through a dedicated pursuit of art and the natural world also signifies the possibilities of alternative mothering practices which can create transformative changes in the sufferer by channelling her disappointment into triumph.

References

Becker, Gay. 1997. *Healing the Infertile Family: Strengthening your Relationship in the Search for Parenthood*. Berkeley, CA: University of California Press.

Carel, Havi. 2007. "Can I Be Ill and Happy." *Philosophia* 35: 95–110. doi:10.1007/s11406-007-908-5.

Carel, Havi. 2013. "Illness, Phenomenology, and Philosophical Method." *Theoretical Medicine and Bioethics* 34(4). 345–357. doi:10.1007/s11017-013-9265-1.
Carel, Havi. 2016. *Phenomenology of Illness*. Oxford: Oxford University Press.
Folkman, Susan. 2008. "The Case for Positive Emotions in the Stress Process." *Anxiety, Stress, and Coping: An International Journal* 21(1): 3–14. doi:10.1080/10615800701740457.
Frank, Arthur. 2002. *At the Will of the Body: Reflections on Illness*. Boston, MA: Mariner Books.
Frankl, Victor E. 1985. *Man's Search for Meaning*. New York: Pocket Books.
Harvard Mental Health Letter. 2009. "The Psychological Impact of Infertility and its Treatment." *Harvard Health*, May. www.health.harvard.edu/newsletter_article/The-psychological-impact-of-infertility-and-its-treatment. Accessed 21 December 2020.
Knight, Paula. 2017. *The Facts of Life*. Oxford: Myriad.
McCarthy, Patrice M. 2008. "Women's Lived Experience of Infertility After Unsuccessful Medical Intervention." *Journal of Midwifery and Women's Health* 53(4): 319–324. doi:10.1016/j.jmwh.2007.11.004.
Moch, S. D. 1989. "Health within Illness: Conceptual Evolution and Practical Possibilities." *Advances in Nursing Science* 11(4): 23–31. doi:10.1097/00012272-198907000-00006.
Potts, Phoebe. 2010. *Good Eggs: A Memoir*. New York: Harper Collins.
Potts, Phoebe. 2011. "In 'Good Eggs' Author Copes with Infertility through Comics." Interview by Meghna Chakrabarti, Radio Boston, 5 January.
Roudsari, Robab Latifnejad, Helen T. Allan, and Pam A. Smith. 2007. "Looking at Infertility through the Lens of Religion and Spirituality: A Review of the Literature." *Human Fertility* 10(3): 141–149. doi:10.1080/14647270601182677.
Roudsari, Robab Latifnejad, Helen T. Allan, and Pam A. Smith. 2014. "Iranian and English Women's Use of Religion and Spirituality as Resources for Coping with Infertility." *Human Fertility* 17(2): 114–123. doi:10.3109/14647273.2014.909610.
Sartre, Jean-Paul. 2003. *Being and Nothingness*. London: Routledge.
Schetter, Christine Dunkel, and Marcl Lobel. 1991. "Psychological Reactions to Infertility." In *Infertility: Perspectives from Stress and Coping Research*, ed. Annette L. Stanton and Christine Dunkel-Schetter, 29–57. New York: Springer.
Southwick, Steven M., George A. Bonanno, Ann S. Masten, Catherine Panter Brick, and Rachel Yehuda. 2014. "Resilience Definitions, Theory, and Challenges: Interdisciplinary Perspectives." *European Journal of Psychotraumatology* 5(1): 1–14. doi:10.3402/ejpt.v5.25338.
Sunwolf, Lawrence R. Frey and Lisa Keranen. 2005. "Rx Story Prescriptions: Healing Effects of Storytelling and Storylistening in the Practice of Medicine." In *Narratives, Health, and Healing: Communication Theory, Research, and Practice*, ed. Lynn M. Harter, Phyllis M. Japp, and Christina S. Beck, 237–257. New York: Routledge.

Toombs, S. Kay. 1988. "Illness and the Paradigm of Lived Body." *Theoretical Medicine* 9(2): 201–226. doi:10.1007/BF00489413.

Venkatesan, Sathyaraj, and Chinmay Murali. 2020. "Drawing Infertility: An Interview with Paula Knight, Jenell Johnson, Emily Steinberg, and Phoebe Potts." *Journal of Graphic Novels and Comics.* doi: 10.1080/21504857.2020.1764074

Yorks, Lyle, and Elizabeth Kasl. 2006. "I Know More than I Can Say: A Taxonomy for Using Expressive Ways of Knowing to Foster Transformative Learning." *Journal of Transformative Education* 4(1): 43–64. doi: 10.1177/1541344605283151.

Conclusion

As an interdisciplinary endeavour that strives to interrogate dominant methods of scholarship in health care that are predominantly objective and fact driven, graphic medicine offers an inclusive perspective of health, illness, and medicine. In so doing, the field has created a unique discourse that rejects the notion of a universal patient. Instead, it embraces a broader understanding of sufferers as multiple subjects with varied and often conflicting experiences. Graphic pathographies on various illness conditions have challenged the medical hegemony by bringing the marginal and incidental voice of the patients to the centre of the medical discourse. Furthermore, inspired by the principles of narrative medicine and health humanities movement, graphic medicine underscores the significance of social determinants of health in shaping the experience of illness. Taking these cues, this study examines select women's graphic pathographies on involuntary childlessness and illustrates how these narratives foreground the physical and psychological ordeals of experiencing infertility.

The medical and societal discourses surrounding infertility, the study argues, are mostly centred on the female body and subjectivity. Despite infertility being a gender-neutral health issue, women are often held responsible for the couples' inability to reproduce. The socio-cultural valorisation of motherhood, which is characterised by the entwining of maternity and femininity, mandates women to reproduce. Therefore, women who are unable to bear a child face social stigmatisation and cultural derision. This ideological dictate of enforced motherhood aggravates women's infertility experience as the sufferers internalise the maternal mandate and perceive themselves as incomplete and unfulfilled. Infertility is an ordinary condition; however, it is politicized, medicalised, and configured as a state of perpetual crisis. This discursive reconfiguration of childlessness as 'a medical problem' or a disease

DOI: 10.4324/9781003028628-7

affects women the most. Women are the focus of most treatments even when their partner has fertility issues.

This study, as such, focuses on the gendered nature of infertility experience as delineated in the graphic memoirs chosen for analysis. Apart from foregrounding the gendered and tabooed experience of infertility, the book aims to establish motherhood as an ideological construct shaped by pronatal discourses. At another level, the study attempts to examine how the memoirists exploit the verbal-visual vocabulary and affordances of comics to externalise the affective and lived realities of experiencing involuntary childlessness. Here it is also argued that visual autopathographies are a significant addition to the growing body of life narratives on illness and disability, and particularly to women's auto somatographies. In so doing, the study emphasises the complex interrelationship between women's life writing and graphic medicine. Additionally, the book identifies a growing corpus of graphic memoirs on women's reproductive quandaries and coins the term "gynographics" to denote this subgenre of graphic medicine that addresses various issues related to women's reproduction. Gynographics, in its unique attention to women's reproductive quandaries such as infertility, miscarriage, abortion, postpartum depression, and menopause, differs from other graphic pathographies that focus on women's illness conditions such as breast cancer and eating disorders. Foregrounding the phenomenological and lived perspectives on female reproductive disorders, gynographics lends visibility to women's unarticulated traumas which are usually side-lined, glossed over, and silenced. In other words, these verbal-visual texts demonstrate graphic medicine's potential to create "a discursive and visual forum where the affective, biological, social, and political complexities of reproduction can exist together in generative uncertainty" (Johnson 2018, 4). Among such narratives, women's graphic memoirs on infertility visually and discursively present childless women's psychic and somatic tribulations in a pronatal cultural scape. This study is the first of its kind that explores the representation of infertility in gynographics.

Broadly categorised as women's graphic memoirs on infertility, the primary texts chosen for analysis are Jenell Johnson's *Present/Perfect* (2018), Paula Knight's *The Facts of Life* (2017), Emily Steinberg's *Broken Eggs* (2014), and Phoebe Potts' *Good Eggs* (2010). Despite different aesthetic and thematic concerns, the memoirs chosen for study address the tribulations of involuntary childlessness. Before attempting an analysis of comic narratives, the study theoretically establishes the fundamentals of graphic medicine. The book not only approaches graphic medicine as an offshoot of narrative medicine and medical humanities movement, but also examines graphic pathographies as an addition to life narratives on illness. Alternatively, the study accentuates the potential of graphic medicine in community formation, awareness creation, and offering cathartic relief to sufferers. Graphic medicine's critique of biomedicine forms an integral part of the study. An attempt is also made to document the growing popularity of graphic medicine around the world. Further, the book addresses the politics of representations in the context of female infertility. Here the book examines diverse pop-cultural media representations of women's childlessness and notes that such representations are mostly stereotypical, stigmatising, and misleading. In this backdrop, the study illustrates the potential of women's memoirs to counteract stigmatising and stereotyping popular images of infertility through the portrayal of lived and experiential perspectives. Recognising the power of personal narratives to create a counter-discourse, the book approaches women's graphic memoirs as carrying out the cultural task of destigmatising female infertility in the verbal-visual medium of comics.

The ensuing sections of the book lay bare how women's graphic memoirs critique not only the mainstream socio-cultural discourses for perpetuating pronatal ideology but also the discourses and practices of reproductive medicine for its misogynistic, dehumanising, and estranging tendencies that affect the sufferers adversely. In a close reading of Knight's *The Facts of Life*, the study demonstrates how an uncritical conflation of maternity and womanhood causes severe damage to infertile women's selfhood. The study explores how Knight's narrative exposes the socially constructed and gendered nature of motherhood by foregrounding the role of popular culture, and social apparatuses such as family and education in creating pronatal subjectivities. The book recognises a voice of self-affirmation and defiance emerging from the narrator towards the end of the text. The protagonist denounces the narrow social labelling of women based on their maternal status and affirms her identity as an independent woman free of the shackles of restrictive maternal ideologies. Furthermore, the study draws theoretical templates from the feminist critique of medicalisation to emphasise the patriarchal and misogynist ethos that undergird medical attitudes towards female infertility. Close reading the infertility memoirs chosen for analysis, the book demonstrates how the memoirists bring into sharp relief their dehumanising experiences of hurt and estrangement in the medical encounter. Thematically, while Steinberg and Johnson lament medical apathy and relentless technologization of reproductive medicine, Potts and Knight emphasise the shameful and depersonalising nature of the medical encounter. The study also underscores the ways

Conclusion 109

in which each author exploits the visual-verbal affordances of comics to accentuate their predicament inside the clinic. For instance, Steinberg deploys capitalisation, and repetition of phrases for emphasis and draws herself as a fertility guinea pig trapped inside a cage which symbolises the clinic. Similar techniques could be found in Knight's narrative when the protagonist's reproductive apparatus is visualised as caught inside the comic gutter. As such, the book argues that graphic medicine offers a unique verbal-visual vocabulary for artists to demonstrate the misogynistic, dehumanising, hurtful, and estranging nature of the clinical experience of infertility.

Finally, the book close reads the concluding sections of *The Facts of Life* and *Good Eggs* to illustrate how the memoirists positively come to terms with their infertile subjectivity. In order to overcome the affective challenges of childlessness, both Knight and Potts refashion their identity and priorities, thereby adopting a resilient coping practice. Additionally, the authors reinvent their values and existential goals in their effort to find meaning and hope in their childless existence. While Potts draws sustenance through Jewish spirituality and storytelling practices, Knight affirms her interest in ecology and artistic creativity. Again, Knight's dedicated pursuit of art and the natural world also signifies the possibility of adopting alternative mothering practices which can transcend the constraints of biological motherhood. In sum, the study foregrounds Knight and Potts' resilient subjectivities and their coping strategies to demonstrate the possibility of a successful coping practice in the context of female infertility.

After illustrating how the selected women's graphic pathographies foreground the authors' lived experiences of infertility in its inherent complexity, the study concludes that graphic medicine offers a creative space for artists to externalise their hitherto marginal perspectives on childlessness. Reiterating the subversive legacy of comics and the empowering potential of graphic medicine, the study concludes that visual autopathographies are a suitable mode for articulating the often gendered, tabooed, and silenced experiential realities of women's infertility. The memoirists use the visual aesthetic of comics to document the personal, medical, and socio-cultural challenges of experiencing infertility with force and urgency. In so doing, these artists illustrate that "the representation of the self in the visual comics form is an inherently political undertaking, especially when it comes to bodies and subjectivities that are socially marginalised" (Køhlert 2019, 189).

In sum, the book recognises the power of graphic medicine explicitly to accord visibility and legibility to women's marginal perspectives on childlessness which are often overlooked by the socio-cultural mainstream. Graphic memoirs not only offer a nonthreatening and liberating space for infertile women to externalise their ordeals but also perform a cultural role of counteracting stigmas and steretypes surrounding female infertility.

References

Johnson, Jenell. 2018. "Introduction." In *Graphic Reproduction: A Comics Anthology*, ed. Jenell Johnson, 1–16. University Park: Pennsylvania State University Press.

Køhlert, Byrn Frederik. 2019. *Serial Selves: Identity and Representation in Autobiographical Comics*. New Brunswoick, NJ: Rutgers University Press.

Index

Note: Page numbers in *italics* indicate figures and in **bold** indicate tables on the corresponding pages.

Abortion Eve 24
abortions 24
advertising, egg-freezing 42–43
AIDS and Its Metaphors 37
Alden, P. 46
Alexander-Taner, R. 2
All of a Piece: A Life with Multiple Sclerosis 21, 23
Althusser, L. 56
Alzheimer's Disease 38
Andrews, E. 16
artistic creativity and identity 99–101, *100*
Art of Waiting: On Fertility, Medicine, and Motherhood, The 46
assisted reproductive technology (ART) 74–75
At the Will of the Body: Reflections on Illness 97–98
Atwood, M. 39
autobiographic gynographics 2–3, 107–108; women's life writing and 23–25
autopathography 21–23

Baby Binder: How Unexplained Infertility Forced me to Take Charge of my Life, Health and Medical Treatment so that I Could Live Better and Make Babies, The 46, 47
baby dolls 56

Baby Matrix, The 53
Baby Story, A 43
Baby Trail, The 39–40
Bad Doctor, The 2
Ball, R. 24
Barnes, L. W. 7
Beauvoir, S. de 56
Becker, G. 5
Becoming 1
Behuniak, S. M. 38
Bergen, D. 39
Big Skinny: How I Changed My Fattitude, The 25
biocultural model of illness 36–38
Bleakley, A. 16
body shaming 25
Body Silent, The 21
Boer, M. L. D. 43
Boggs, B. 46
breast cancer 24–25
Broken Eggs 8, 29, 71, 76–83, *77*, *80*, 87, 107
Brookes, T. 22
Butler, J. 56

Canadian Association for Health Humanities 18–19
Cancer Journals, The 21
Cancer Made Me A Shallower Person: A Memoir 24
Cancer Vixen: A True Story 22, 24, 29

Carel, H. 98
Carroll, L. 53
Cartwright, L. 82
Castro, R. de 73
Catching My Breath: An Asthmatic Explores his Illness 22
Charon, R. 19–20
Chevely, L. 24
childlessness: cultural otherhood and 60–64, *63*; as tool of self-discovery 102
Children of Men, The 39
Chori Chori Chupke Chupke 40
Chute, H. 23–24
Clarke, C. 45
Cohen, L. 44
Comics and Sequential Art 9
Conceivability: What I Learned Exploring the Frontiers of Fertility 46, 47
Conception Story, A 44
Couser, G. 21, 22–23
Couser, T. 47
Coxon, C. 57–58
Crawford, P. 19
Crazy Hospital 29
Crossing the Moon: A Journey through Infertility 46
cultural censoring 1
cultural otherhood 60–64, *63*
cultural representations of women's infertility 106–107; biocultural model of illness and 36–38; countering infertile subjectivity in women's memoirs and 45–47; egg-freezing ads and rhetoric of choice in 42–43; as infertile monsters in reality TV, and horror films 43–45; introduction to 35; in popular novels and mass-market women's magazines 38–40; self-blame and neurosis in TV melodrama 40–42; significance of 47–48
Czerwiec, M. K. 2, 3, 26, 28

Dahl, K. 2, 26
Dally, A. 83
Daly, M. 76
Davis, L. J. 25
Davis-Floyd, R. 72

Debeurme, L. 25
Degrassi 38
"Depersonalisation of Women through the Administration of 'In Vitro Fertilisation,' The" 75
Disease and Representation: Images of Illness from Madness to AIDS 36
Disrepute 26
Dumb: Living without a Voice 2
Dunlap-Shohl, P. 29

Edge, B. 40, 41–42, 44
egg-freezing ads 42–43
Eisner, W. 9
El Refaie, E. 78
Empire 38
Engelberg, M. 24

Facts of Life, The 2, 8, 52, 54, 71, 87, 91, 103, 107, 109; art, ecology, and alternative mothering practices in 97–102, *100*; childlessness and cultural otherhood in 60–64, *63*; girl child as pronatalist subject in *55*, 55–60, *59*; thinking beyond motherhood in 64–67, *68*; trauma and embarrassment in fertility care in 83–85, *85*
Fairfield, L. 25
Farmer, J. 24, 26
Fatal Attraction 38
feminine beauty and embodiment 24–25
feminism 54; critique of medicalisation 71–76, 87–88
Ferrier, T. 26
Fies, B. 2, 22, 29, 30
Flexner, A. 17
Forney, E. 29
Fosket, J. R. 38
Foucault, M. 72
Fountain, L. 24
Frank, A. 97–98
Frankl, V. 102
Fransman, K. 25
From Here to Maternity 39
Fussell, T. 24

Ganev, R. 39
Gardien, C.-M. 73

Gaviola, K. 41
gender and infertility 5–7
Gilman, S. L. 36
Glazer, S. 29
"Goldie: A Neurotic Woman" 24
Good Eggs 2, 8, 27, 71, 91, 103, 107, 109; critique of medicalisation in 85–87; spiritual and creative coping with infertility in 94–97
Grace 44
graphic medicine 2–3, 106–110; aims, objectives, and methodology on 8–10; data for analysis on 8; humanising healthcare through 16–19; internationalisation and popularisation of 29–31; introduction to 15–16; narrative medicine relationship to 20–21; as pedagogical tool 25–27; as therapy, community, and critique 27–29; women's life writing and 23–25
Graphic Medicine Manifesto 20–21, 27
graphic pathography 21–23, 106
"Graphic Storytelling and Medical Narratives" 26
Green, K. 25, 27, 28
Green, M. J. 22, 26
Greil, A. 7, 73
Grey's Anatomy 40–41
Groensteen, T. 9–10
Guardian, The 29
gynographics 2–3; data for analysis on 8

Hall, S. 37
Haller, J. S. 7
Haller, R. M. 7
Halloween 38
Handmaid's Tale 39
Harrison, T. 24
Hawkins, A. H. 21
Hayden, J. 24
health humanities 17–19
Health Humanities Consortium in the US 18
Heidegger, M. 81
HIV and AIDS 37
Holmgren, L. 19–20

Homeland 38
homosexuality 23–24
horror films 43–45
House that Groaned, The 25
humanising of healthcare 16–19

ideology 56
illness: as dangerous opportunity 97–98; pregnancy as 72–73; representations of 36–38
Illness as Metaphor 37
In-Between Days 24
Incredible Facts O' Life Sex Education Funnies 24
"Infertile Bodies: Medicalisation, Metaphor, and Agency" 73
infertility: acceptance of 98–99, 103; art, ecology, and alternative mothering practices in 97–102, *100*; cultural representations of women's 35–48; defining 3–4; as disease 4–5; gender and 5–7; in popular novels and mass-market women's magazines 38–40; resilience, coping, and infertile subjectivity with 91–93, 102–103; social construction of experience of 6–7; spiritual and creative coping with 94–97, 109; statistics on 4; in television melodramas 40–42
Infertility: History of a Transformative Term 6
Inflatable Woman, The 24
Inhorn, M. C. 6
Ink in Water: An Illustrated Memoir (Or, How I Kicked Anorexia's Ass and Embraced Body Positivity) 25
Inside Out: Portrait of an Eating Disorder 25
International Health Humanities Network in the UK 18
internationalisation and popularisation of graphic medicine 29–31
In vitro 9
in vitro fertilization (IF) 75
It Ain't Me Babe: Women's Liberation 23
It's Alive 44

James, P. D. 39
Japan Graphic Medicine Association (JGMA) 29–30
Jayabalan, R. 1
Jayadevan, A. 46–47
Jenkins, T. 45–46
Jensen, R. E. 6–7
Johnson, J. 8, 71, 80–83, 87, 107, 108
Johnson, M. A. 37
Jones, T. 18

Kate & Jon Plus 8 43
Katkin, E. 46, 47
Keith, M. 79
Kesavan, M. 1
Kettner, J. 25
Klugman, C. 17–18
Knight, P. 2, 8, 68–69, 71, 87, 91, 103, 107, 108–109; *see also Facts of Life, The*
Køhlert, F. B. 24
Kominsky-Crumb, A. 24
Krüger-Fürhoff, I. M. 30

Lalanda, M. 30
Lay, C. 25
Leg to Stand On, A 21
Leviatt, S. 28
life writing 21–23; quality of 47; women's 23–25, 45–47
Lighter than My Shadow 25, 27
Little Couple, The 44
Lorde, A. 21
Loughran, T. 38–39
Lucille 25
Lupton, D. 37

Mairs, N. 23
Malicious Medicine: My Experience with Fraud and Falsehood in Infertility Clinics 46–47
Mammoir: A Pictorial Odyssey of the Adventures of a Fourth Grade Teacher with Breast Cancer 24
Marbles: Mania, Depression, Michelangelo & Me 29
Marchetto, M. A. 22, 24, 29
Markle, M. 1

Marsh, M. 41
Martin, E. 72
mass-market women's magazines, infertile women in 38–40
May, E. 5, 7
McCloud, S. 9–10
McLean, T. 22
Medical Education in the United States and Canada: A Report to the Carnegie Foundation for the Advancement of Teaching 17
medical gaze 72–73
medical humanities 16–19
medicalisation: apathetic/exploitive infertility care and 76–83, *77, 80*; embarrassment and trauma in fertility care and 83–87, *85*; feminist critique of 71–76, 87–88; introduction to 71
Menopause: A Comic Treatment 2
mental illness, representations of 38
Micks, C. 46, 47
Mom's Cancer 2, 22, 29, 30
Monsters 2, 26
monsters, infertile women portrayed as 43–45
Moriarty, S. 39
Morris, D. B. 36
motherhood, social construction of 52–54
Motherhoodwinked: An Infertility Memoir 46, 47
Mr Jones 38
Munthe, E. G. 37
Murali, C. 97, 102
Murphy, R. 21
My Degeneration: A Journey though Parkinson's 29
Myers, K. R. 22

Nachtigall, R. D. 5
narrative medicine 19–21
Noe, M. 30
Notkin, M. 53

Obama, M. 1
objectification 25
Overwhelmed, Anxious and Angry: Navigating Postpartum Depression 2

Passing for Normal: A Memoir of Compulsion 22
pathographies 21–23
Peck, E. 52, 54
pedagogical tool, graphic medicine as 25–27
Perfect Match, A 39
Physician and Sexuality in Victorian America, The 7
Pinheiro, C. 73
Plaintext 23
popular novels, infertile women in 38–40
Potts, P. 2, 8, 27, 71, 85–87, 91, 103, 107, 108–109; spiritual and creative coping with infertility in 94–97
pregnancy treated as illness 72–73
Present/Perfect 8, 71, 80–83, 87, 107
Pretending to be Normal: Living with Asperger's Syndrome 22
Private Life 45
Private Practice 40–41
Prometheus 44–45
pronatalism: childlessness and cultural otherhood versus 60–64, *63*; introduction to 52; Knight's girl child as pronatalist subject and 55, 55–60, *59*; social construction of motherhood and 52–54; thinking beyond motherhood and 64–67, *68*; see also *Facts of Life, The*
Pronatalism: The Myth of Mom and Apple Pie 52

quality of life writing 47

Rattled 43
reality television 43–45
Reinke, E. E. 17
resilience and coping with infertility 91–93, 102–103
rhetoric of choice 42–43
Robbins, T. 23
Rodgers, J. 53–54
Romberge, J. 29
Romer, W. 41
Roney, L. 22
Roy, W. 9

Sacks, O. 21
Sandelowski, M. J. 6, 7
Sarton, G. 16
Sartre, J.-P. 92
Schulz, G. 29
Scott, R. 44
Scully, A.-M. 46, 47
Second Sex, The 56
Seized: My Life with Epilepsy 22
self-blame 40–42
Senderowitz, J. 52, 54
7 Miles a Second 29
Sex and the City 40, 41
Shaw, J. 72–73
Shepherd, E. 2
Shivack, N. 25
Showalter, E. 3
Sick 29
Siegel, F. 16
Significant Loss: The Story of My Miscarriage, A 2
Sims, D. 45
Singh, S. 30
Small, D. 2, 27, 29
Snitow, A. 52, 54
social construction of motherhood 52–54
Solet, P. 44
Sontag, S. 37
Spallone, P. 74–75
Special Exits 26
spiritual and creative coping 94–97, 109
Squier, S. M. 28, 30
Steinberg, D. 72, 75, 108–109
Steinberg, E. 8, 29, 71, 87, 107, 108; *Broken Eggs* 76–83, *77, 80*
Stitches 2, 27
Story of My Tits, The 24
storytelling 96–97
Stranger 39
Sunwolf, L. R. 97
Sweet Invisible Body: Reflections on a Life with Diabetes 22
System of Comics, The 10

television melodramas 40–42
Tits 'n' Clits 24
Tyranny 25
Tzu-Yao, L. 29

Understanding Comics: The Invisible Art 9

van Balen, F. 6
Venkatesan, S. 30, 97, 102
visualising of illness: autopathography, graphic pathography, and life writing in 21–23; comics, graphic medicine, and women's life writing in 23–25; graphic medicine as pedagogical tool in 25–27; graphic medicine as therapy, community, and critique in 27–29; humanising healthcare and 16–19; internationalisation and popularisation of graphic medicine and 29–31; introduction to 15–16; narrative medicine in 19–21

Webber, G. 2
Webster, B. 21, 23
Wilensky, A. 22
Willey, L. H. 22
Williams, I. 2, 20–21, 27, 28
Williamson, R. 43
Wimmin's Comix 23
Wojnarowicz, D. 29
women's health 24
women's life writing 23–25; countering infertile subjectivity 45–47

Zucker, J. 2

Milton Keynes UK
Ingram Content Group UK Ltd.
UKHW020631280124
436834UK00003B/3